PUBLISHING

A Wild Australia Guide

SHARKS & RAYS

DR TONY AYLING & STEVE PARISH

Contents

Introduction

Sharks and rays are an exciting group of fish. These amazing animals belong to the class Chondrichthyes and include the three largest fish in the oceans as well as many sharks that are able to kill and eat humans! Excitement and fear are the two emotions most often evoked by these animals but with a bit of knowledge it is possible to add respect to that list.

Sharks and rays are distinctive in having a skeleton that is made out of cartilage; a material that is softer than bone. Ancestral sharks and rays apparently had bony skeletons but this was lost and replaced with lighter cartilage (to save weight and improve buoyancy control) early in their evolution. Sharks and rays differ from bony fish by having small tooth-like scales called dermal denticles embedded in their skin and having teeth that are buried in their gums, instead of attached to their jaws. These teeth are constantly replaced and most sharks have several rows of developing teeth behind the main row. Sharks and rays are also unusual in having their mouth and nostrils on the underside of their head (rather than at the front); they also lack the buoyancy control swim bladder possessed by most bony fish. Male sharks and rays have claspers that are used to grasp females during mating, to insert sperm into the female's cloaca. Cartilaginous fish all have internal fertilisation of their eggs and either give birth to live young or lay a few large eggs. There are about 1000 shark and ray species worldwide and almost 300 of these are found in Australian waters.

IDENTIFYING SHARKS IN THE FIELD

To identify a shark we need to calmly check a number of features. First look at the body shape and colour and try to objectively estimate the shark's size. Next check the tail shape and size as well as the number, shape, relative height and colour markings of the dorsal fins. Finally, take note of the number and size of the gill slits and the size and colour of the shark's eye.

Top, left: *Urolophus* sp., an undescribed stingaree from south-eastern Australia.
Above, top to bottom: Brown-banded Bamboo Shark (*Chiloscyllium punctatum*) — juvenile, teenager and adult.

THROUGH AEONS OF TIME

Sharks are an ancient group. The first sharks evolved in the Silurian Period about 435 million years ago and looked remarkably similar to some modern species. These animals were such an instant evolutionary success that their body form and lifestyle have changed very little over several hundred million years. Though the relatively soft cartilaginous skeleton of sharks does not fossilise easily, their teeth preserve well. Fossil shark teeth are extremely abundant and many of them look almost identical to the teeth of modern sharks. The illustrated fossil shark tooth (right) comes from a close relative of the White Shark that patrolled warm seas 2- 25 million years ago. Known as the Megatooth Shark (*Carcharodon megalodon*), this awesome predator had teeth over 15 cm long and was a whale-eating giant, growing to a length of 15 m and weighing over 35 t!

FEATURES OF A SHARK

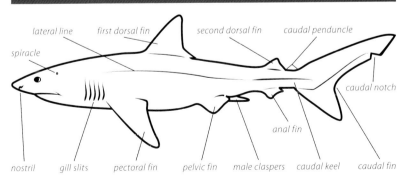

lateral line · first dorsal fin · second dorsal fin · caudal penduncle · spiracle · caudal notch · anal fin · nostril · gill slits · pectoral fin · pelvic fin · male claspers · caudal keel · caudal fin

Shark Senses

Everyone knows that a shark has an amazingly acute sense of smell, but its complete sensory capability is extremely sophisticated.

VISION: Sharks have excellent vision, with better contrast detection and sensitivity than human eyes. They have both cones and rods in their retinas and see in high-contrast colour. A mirror-like surface behind the eye reflects received light back through the retina and doubles the eye's sensitivity. Many predatory sharks rely on sight — more than other senses — for hunting.

HEARING: Sharks not only hear sounds as we do, but also feel very low frequency vibrations such as those emitted by a struggling fish. They have internal ears (similar to our own) on each side of the top of the head, with a small hole to the exterior. This enables them to hear lower frequencies than humans. While humans hear sounds from about 25–16,000 Hz (cycles per second), the range for sharks is 10–800 Hz. Sharks also "hear" the ripples and vibrations caused by swimming fish or water movements. This is made possible by a tubular lateral line canal system containing many tiny hair cells called neuromasts — similar to those inside a vertebrate's inner ear.

SMELL: Shark nostrils are sensitive to minute traces of many chemicals (not just blood). The nasal passages are large and open through nostrils set wide apart on the underside of the head. This separation creates slight differences in smell intensity in each nostril, and so lets sharks determine the direction from which a particular odour is emanating. Almost 20% of a shark's brain is used for processing smell information.

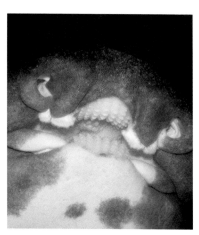

Top, left: A White Shark sniffing the surface slick. **Above:** Bottom-feeding sharks like the Port Jackson Shark have complex sensory pits near the mouth and nostrils for detecting prey.

TASTE: Taste organs in the shark's mouth and throat help it to decide whether something is edible or not. Some sharks are fussy eaters and will reject items that taste bad or are not sufficiently energy-rich.

TOUCH: Pressure receptors all over the shark's skin let it detect touch.

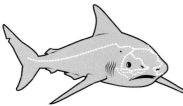

Top: As well as having sensitive eyes and nostrils, sharks have an array of electrical sensing pits around the nose and head, visible as small black dots on the head of this White Shark (also see enlarged inset, right). **Above:** The lateral line is a series of fluid-filled canals that sense low-frequency vibrations.

ELECTRORECEPTION: Sharks have an important sixth sense that enables them to detect the extremely faint electrical fields that surround all living creatures. The "ampullae of Lorenzini" are numerous small electrical sense organs scattered over the head. It is thought that these sense organs can also detect the current generated by a shark's movement through the Earth's magnetic field. This may assist with navigation.

Shark Conservation

Sharks are under assault by the modern fishing industry. It is estimated that over 100 million sharks are killed each year throughout the world — a number that has increased dramatically since the 1960s. In Australia about 10,000 t of sharks are caught annually, which probably equates to five million individuals. Many sharks and rays are caught for food but a distressing number are discarded after their high-value fins are cut off. Dried shark fins fetch about $100 per kilogram on the Asian market. Large sharks are also caught to have their jaws removed, and these are sold as souvenirs. Because the lifestyles of sharks and rays are very different from that of bony fish, they are even more sensitive to fishing pressure. Manta Rays give birth every two years to a single offspring, and probably only produce 5–6 young in an entire lifetime. Most sharks are slow growing and do not mature until they are 10–12 years old. Females give birth (on average) every two years to a few large young. Many sharks only produce a life total of 10–30 offspring and even the most fecund species such as the Tiger and Blue Sharks probably only have a few hundred pups during their lives. As a result, shark populations are quickly depleted by any sustained commercial-level catch. Most shark fisheries provide good returns for a few years and then decline rapidly unless the effort is shifted to another place or to another species. Even well-managed fisheries seldom remain viable in the long term. Sharks are important predators in most ecosystems — we do not yet know the long-term effect of the removal of so many of these large, top-level carnivores from the oceans.

Top, left: Dried shark fins fetch high prices in the Asian markets. **Above:** Alf Dean with his world-record White Shark catch. Before they were protected, these huge sharks were sought after by sport fishers. **Opposite:** In the 1960s divers killed many whaler sharks to protect swimmers from these perceived "man-eaters".

Shark Attack

KEEPING IT IN PERSPECTIVE: The thought of being eaten by a shark terrifies most people. Many Australians will not go swimming because of the risk of being attacked by a shark. The old joke about not swimming in the shark's ocean if it doesn't swim in my bath is very true for some of us! But it is important to put this danger into perspective. Each year hundreds of thousands of Australians swim or dive in the sea — but on average only one person a year dies from a shark attack in Australia. This compares with: one death a year from crocodile attacks; two deaths from lightning strikes; two from bee stings; two from surfboard accidents; nine from diving accidents; 320 from drowning, and over 2500 deaths from motor vehicle accidents! Family dogs kill more people each year than sharks. Getting into a car is certainly more risky than getting into the sea with sharks but we don't fear cars or want to "kill" them!

As the table below shows, even if you were to be attacked by a shark you probably have a better than 50% chance of survival. In many states the incidence of fatal attacks is less than 30%.

Top, left: Many attacks result from sharks excited by spearfishing activities. **Above:** Shark meshing off Australian beaches kills many large sharks each year.

TOTAL SHARK ATTACKS & FATALITIES OVER A 200 YEAR PERIOD
(Data collected by the Australian Shark Attack File)

TOTAL ATTACKS	STATE	FATAL ATTACKS	PERCENTAGE FATAL
244	NSW	72	29.5%
228	QLD	72	31.6%
34	VIC	7	20.5%
50	SA	21	42.0%
79	WA	13	16.5%
12	NT	3	25.0%
21	TAS	5	28.9%

Shark Size

Modern sharks exist in a huge range of sizes. Thankfully, the largest sharks are harmless. Whale Sharks, the gentle giants of the shark world, grow to over 18 m in length and weigh more than 35 t. Basking Sharks, filter-feeders of colder waters, are also massive — growing to a length of 10 m. Manta Rays may be over 6 m across and weigh 1.5 t. The largest of the dangerous sharks are the White, Tiger and Great Hammerhead Sharks, which all grow to about 6 m long. On the other hand, over half of Australia's shark species do not grow to more than 1 m in length. The smallest shark is the tiny Pygmy Shark that survives in the open ocean and is only 20 cm long when fully grown. However, it is difficult to estimate the size of a shark accurately and many myths have grown regarding the maximum size of large sharks. Even when a shark has been caught, it is not often accurately measured.

Above: Measuring a large shark accurately is a difficult process. **Below:** Relative sizes of various shark species next to an adult human.

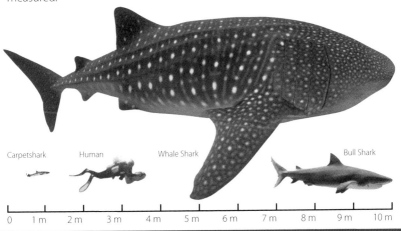

Carpetshark   Human   Whale Shark   Bull Shark

| 0 | 1 m | 2 m | 3 m | 4 m | 5 m | 6 m | 7 m | 8 m | 9 m | 10 m |

The Science of Sharks

AGE & GROWTH: It is difficult to study sharks, especially the larger, more wide-ranging species. As a first step, standard fishery biology methods can be applied to sharks that have been caught. Examination of stomach contents reveals much about shark diets, and the age of most sharks can be estimated by cutting cross-sections of their vertebrae or fin spines and counting rings. Recapture of measured, tagged sharks can also give us information on how rapidly sharks grow and how long they live, but recaptures are usually few and far between.

REPRODUCTION: Dissection of captured sharks can also reveal how they breed. The only information available on the reproduction of the rare Whale Shark comes from the examination of a single large pregnant female that was killed in the Taiwanese shark fishery. This is not a very productive method as many of the sharks captured are immature or are males. Such studies usually only give hints about the length of pregnancy and where sharks go to mate and give birth.

BEHAVIOUR & LEARNING: Diving studies have been made of the behaviour of sedentary sharks such as the Port Jackson Shark but how can we study the behaviour of a large ocean-roaming predator? Laboratory and aquarium experiments have shown that sharks can learn quickly and remember lessons for a long time. We now know that they are far from merely being dumb, instinct-driven killing machines.

Top: A researcher holds a pop-up satellite tag used for tracking sharks.
Above: Researchers measure and weigh a captured White Shark.
Opposite: Underwater electronic radio sensor used to count the passage of tagged Greynurse Sharks.

INDIVIDUAL IDENTIFICATION: In the last decade, exciting new techniques have been developed that do not rely on killing or confining sharks in order to study them. Photo identification of individual sharks has started to reveal interesting facts on the lifestyles and behaviour of White Sharks and Whale Sharks, but this is a slow process.

SATELLITE TAGGING: Many studies are now underway to put GPS tags on sharks and rays but this is an expensive and time-consuming process. Tiger Sharks, White Sharks, Manta Rays and other species are now beaming up signals to satellites that offer us tantalising glimpses of their remarkable lives. A White Shark tagged in South Africa recently crossed to Australia and back to South Africa in about nine months, travelling a distance of 22,000 km!

MONITORING STATIONS: Pulse transmitters that send signals to an array of underwater monitoring receivers have been inserted into sharks. This gives researchers a day-to-day view of the movement of individuals and tells us a lot about their lives. However, all the work carried out to date has barely scratched the surface of what there is to know about the exciting world of sharks and rays.

Sharks

Sharks and rays are all in the class Chondrichthyes (cartilaginous fish) but this large group is subdivided into about fourteen orders. Scientists often disagree on the number of orders and how they should be arranged (the number of proposed orders ranges from 10–17). The order arrangement is based on lots of features, many of which relate to internal anatomy, so it is sometimes difficult to see the relationships that distinguish the different groups. For example, the small harmless catsharks are included in the order Carchariniformes along with the Tiger Shark and all the whaler sharks. In other groups, the relationships are more obvious. The sixgill and sevengill sharks are all included together in the Hexanchiformes, while the sedentary bullhead sharks are in their own order (Heterodontiformes). Two other unusual groups, the angelsharks and the sawsharks, are also given their own orders and these, as well as the Squaliformes, all lack an anal fin. The Lamniformes includes many similar, active, warm-blooded sharks, while the diverse order Orectolobiformes includes many different shark types (such as the bottom-living wobbegongs and the huge Whale Shark).

Frilled Shark
Chlamydoselachus anguineus

Frilled Sharks are unmistakeable, with: an elongated eel-like body; a snake-like head with a huge mouth; and six large, frilly gill slits characteristic of the order Hexanchiformes (sixgill and sevengill sharks). The first pair of gill slits meets beneath the throat, much like those of a typical bony fish. Frilled Sharks have huge, wide-opening jaws with distinctive three-pointed teeth. A single small dorsal fin, as well as pelvic and anal fins, are close together near the tail.

DESCRIPTION: Frilled Sharks are a uniform dark chocolate-brown in colour. Unlike most sharks, but like most fish, the Frilled Shark's pectoral fins are rounded and held flat against the body. The tail has a long, pointed upper lobe but no lower lobe.

HABITAT: These sharks live in deep water and are only seen by offshore fishers. They are usually caught in bottom trawls and are thought to hunt on or near the seabed; however, occasional specimens are trapped in open sea gillnets.

BEHAVIOUR: Very little is known of the biology and behaviour of this shark.

FEEDING HABITS: The Frilled Shark has a huge distensible mouth and stomach and can catch and swallow large prey. Frilled Sharks mostly feed on other deepwater sharks.

BREEDING: Frilled Sharks are ovoviviparous with a litter size of 8–15 pups that are born when they are 40–60 cm long.

DANGER TO HUMANS: Frilled Sharks never enter marine habitats frequented by humans but with their small teeth, would be quite harmless if they did.

HABITAT & DISTRIBUTION: Frilled Sharks live near the bottom in water 120–1300 m deep; they are distributed patchily worldwide

SEXUAL MATURITY: M 1.2 m; F 1.4 m

LENGTH: 2 m (max.)

STATUS: Near Threatened (IUCN)

Broadnose Shark *Notorynchus cepedianus*

The Broadnose Shark, often called the Sevengill Shark, is a large species that is easy to identify. This shark has a single dorsal fin set well back on the body and a broad head with a large mouth. The most distinctive feature of the Broadnose Shark is the seven long gill slits (most sharks have only five) that decrease in height from front to back.

DESCRIPTION: Broadnose Sharks are unusually pale in colour, with a fawn or grey back and a white belly. The back and fins are speckled with small black and white spots. The tail has a long upper lobe with a terminal notch and a small lower lobe.

HABITAT: These sharks are bottom-swimming inshore hunters and are often seen close to the coast or in estuaries.

BEHAVIOUR: Broadnose Sharks are active and powerful swimmers.

FEEDING HABITS: These sharks have sharp cutting teeth and feed on a wide range of prey. Favourite targets include other sharks, rays and large and small fish. They also eat seals and sometimes gather in cooperative groups to hunt them.

BREEDING: Broadnose Sharks are ovoviviparous and have large litters of up to 82 pups.

DANGER TO HUMANS: These large sharks are often aggressive to divers or fishers and have been known to bite attendant divers in aquariums. Although they are potentially dangerous, there has never been a verified attack on swimmers or divers in the wild.

HABITAT & DISTRIBUTION: Broadnose Sharks live in coastal waters down to depths of 140 m; found in all temperate seas except the North Atlantic

SEXUAL MATURITY:
M 1.5 m; F 2.2 m
LENGTH:
3 m (max.)
STATUS:
Data Deficient (IUCN)

Port Jackson Sharks are distinctive nocturnal sharks that spend most of the day resting on the bottom. They have a large blunt head (giving rise to the description "Bullhead") with raised bony crests above the eyes and a large deeply notched tail fin. There are sharp venomous spines in front of each of the two equal-sized dorsal fins that help to protect these slow swimmers from larger predators.

DESCRIPTION: Port Jackson Sharks are grey to light brown with a distinct harness-like pattern of darker bands on the body and fins.

HABITAT: These sharks are often found resting in groups in sandy gutters around inshore rocky reefs during the late winter and spring breeding season. They move into deeper water and migrate south during the summer.

BEHAVIOUR: Port Jackson Sharks have been more thoroughly studied than most sharks and each individual has a few preferred resting places. Individuals trapped and moved several kilometres, quickly find their way home.

FEEDING HABITS: The sharp teeth at the front of the jaws are for gripping prey but those at the back are blunt crushing plates. Sea urchins, seastars and molluscs are favourite foods.

BREEDING: After mating, female Port Jackson Sharks lay 10–15 eggs that are about 15 cm long. Females pick up the spiral-flanged eggs and push them into crevices in shallow water where they remain for twelve months until the 20 cm long pups hatch.

DANGER TO HUMANS: Harmless, but care should be taken to avoid the toxic spines if these sharks are handled.

HABITAT & DISTRIBUTION:
Bottom-living on reefs and sand, from shallow water out to over 200 m depth; southern Australia and one record from New Zealand

SEXUAL MATURITY:
M 75 cm; F 85 cm
LENGTH:
1.65 m (max.)
STATUS:
Secure

Crested Hornshark *Heterodontus galeatus*

Crested Hornsharks seem to be all fin. They are similar to Port Jackson Sharks but their fins are much larger and the bony head crests above their eyes are much more pronounced. Their protective dorsal fin spines are less prominent than their relative's and they lack the characteristic "harness" pattern of dark stripes.

DESCRIPTION: Crested Hornsharks are yellow-brown, with several broad dark bars and "saddles".

HABITAT: These sharks are usually seen around rocky reefs in water more than 20 m deep. It is thought they may be more abundant in water beyond diving range.

BEHAVIOUR: Little is known about the lifestyle of these sharks but they probably have a similar behaviour to Port Jackson Sharks.

FEEDING HABITS: The favourite food of Crested Hornsharks is purple sea urchins, but they will also eat crustaceans, molluscs and worms. Strangely, all hornsharks seem to prefer prickly sea urchins to other food.

BREEDING: During winter, females lay large spirally flanged eggs among bottom growths in water 20–30 m deep. These eggs also have sticky tendrils to help attach them to the bottom. The eggs hatch about eight months later when the young are about 20 cm long. These sharks take about twelve years to reach maturity and may live to an age of at least 30 years.

DANGER TO HUMANS: Crested Hornsharks are considered harmless; however, people need to be wary of their dorsal spines!

HABITAT & DISTRIBUTION: Bottom-living, usually around reefs, from close inshore out to 100 m depth; only found in south-east Australia

SEXUAL MATURITY: M 60 cm; F 70 cm (max.)

LENGTH: 1.3 m

STATUS: Secure

Carpetshark Families

Carpetsharks are small elongate sharks that rarely exceed a metre in length. They have two equal-sized dorsal fins on the hind half of the body and a long tail fin with no lower lobe. They have small heads and mouths with numerous tiny sharp teeth in each jaw and a short barbel next to each nostril on the underside of the head.

DESCRIPTION: Carpetsharks are variously patterned with black and white spots.

HABITAT: These sharks live around coral or rocky reefs and are most abundant in shallow water.

BEHAVIOUR: Coral formations or rocky holes and crevices provide hiding places for these sharks during the day. They spend a lot of time resting on the bottom and swim sinuously away, almost touching the bottom, if they are disturbed.

FEEDING HABITS: Carpetsharks feed on a variety of invertebrates, including crabs, shrimps, worms, small sea urchins, octopuses and small fish, that they probably hunt mostly at night.

BREEDING: All these sharks are oviparous. Each year a female lays up to 50 eggs about 10 cm long, which she leaves on the bottom to hatch. It takes about 120 days for the 15–20 cm young to develop and hatch.

DANGER TO HUMANS: Carpetsharks are harmless to humans.

Epaulette Shark *Hemiscyllium ocellatum*

SEXUAL MATURITY: M 60 cm; F 70 cm
LENGTH: 105 cm (max.)
HABITAT & DISTRIBUTION:
Shallow water around coral reefs down to 60 m; only found around New Guinea and in northern Australia
STATUS: Secure

Rusty Carpetshark *Parascyllium ferrugineum*

SEXUAL MATURITY: M 60 cm; F 65 cm

LENGTH: 80 cm (max.)

HABITAT & DISTRIBUTION:
Bottom-dwelling around southern Australia at depths of 5–150 m

STATUS: Secure

Collar Carpetshark *Parascyllium collare*

SEXUAL MATURITY: Not known

LENGTH: 90 cm (max.)

HABITAT & DISTRIBUTION:
Bottom-dwelling in 20–160 m depth; only found between Mooloolaba and Gabo Island

STATUS: Secure

Varied Carpetshark *Parascyllium variolatum*

SEXUAL MATURITY: Not known

LENGTH: 90 cm (max.)

HABITAT & DISTRIBUTION:
Bottom-living in reef and seagrass habitats around southern Australia at depths of 5–180 m

STATUS: Secure

Wobbegong Family

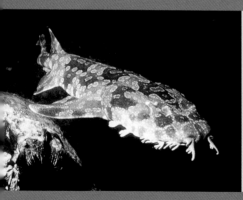

There are about ten species of wobbegong, nine of which are found in Australia; however, some confusion exists about the naming of this group and several species are undescribed. Wobbegongs are all similar bottom-dwelling sharks that have broad, rounded heads with a fringe of skin lobes and a mottled brown and white camouflage colour pattern.

DESCRIPTION: Different wobbegong species are identified by slight variations in colour pattern and in the number and shape of chin lobes.

HABITAT: All wobbegongs live in waters less than 100 m deep on rocky or coral reefs.

BEHAVIOUR: These sharks are nocturnally active, so each individual spends the day resting on the bottom in one of a few favourite sites.

FEEDING HABITS: Wobbegongs are ambush predators that wait for fish or crustaceans to come too close before lunging upwards to engulf them within a large mouth. They will feed during the day, but hunt more actively at night.

BREEDING: These sharks are all ovoviviparous and give birth to young that are about 20 cm long.

DANGER TO HUMANS: Wobbegongs have sharp teeth and have bitten divers who speared or molested them. Wobbegongs hang on tight and can cause serious wounds. Reports of Tasselled Wobbegongs killing people in New Guinea are probably fanciful.

Spotted Wobbegong
Orectolobus maculatus

SEXUAL MATURITY: M 60 cm

LENGTH: 3.0 m (max.)

HABITAT & DISTRIBUTION: Bottom-living shark found from the shore to depths of 110 m around southern Australia; other records doubtful

STATUS: Vulnerable in NSW, Near Threatened through rest of range (IUCN)

Cobbler Wobbegong

Sutorectus tentaculatus

SEXUAL MATURITY: 65 cm

LENGTH: 90 cm (max.)

HABITAT & DISTRIBUTION: Only found around inshore rocky reefs of southern Australia between Adelaide and Carnarvon

STATUS: Secure

Banded Wobbegong

Orectolobus ornatus

SEXUAL MATURITY: 63 cm

LENGTH: 1.5 m (max.)

HABITAT & DISTRIBUTION: Inshore coral and rocky reefs from northern NSW to New Guinea (previously confused with southern *O. halei*)

STATUS: Near Threatened (IUCN)

Tasselled Wobbegong

Eucrossorhinus dasypogon

SEXUAL MATURITY: Not known

LENGTH: 1.4 m (max.)

HABITAT & DISTRIBUTION: Bottom-living on coral reefs around northern Australia and New Guinea

STATUS: Near Threatened (IUCN)

Tawny Sharks are large, sluggish, bottom-dwelling sharks that have two equal-sized dorsal fins set back near the tail and a very long single-lobed tail fin. They have a: blunt head; small eye; an obvious breathing spiracle behind each eye; and the fifth gill slit is set very close to the fourth. There is a pair of barbels alongside the nostrils under the front of the snout.

DESCRIPTION: Tawny sharks are bulky, with a broad head and body with a grey-brown back and paler underparts.

HABITAT: Tawny Sharks live on or near the bottom around coral reefs.

BEHAVIOUR: Tawny Sharks are more active at night and are often seen resting on the bottom in caves or under overhangs during the day, sometimes in groups of two or three individuals.

Unlike most sharks, they swim with their pectoral fins swept upward.

FEEDING HABITS: Tawny Sharks have many small, multi-pointed teeth and feed by using the pharynx as a suction pump to inhale prey. Favourite foods are octopuses and squids, large crustaceans and reef fish.

BREEDING: Tawny Sharks are ovoviviparous. Females retain their egg cases internally until eight young hatch at a length of about 40 cm.

DANGER TO HUMANS: Harmless, but can reverse their pharynx pump to blast a powerful jet of water at tormentors. Divers can often approach resting Tawny Sharks very closely and touch them without reaction. These sharks may become excited in the vicinity of fish-feeding operations and have been known to bump into divers.

HABITAT & DISTRIBUTION:
Tawny Sharks are found in water less than 70 m deep around coral reefs, and are widely distributed in the Indo–Pacific

SEXUAL MATURITY:
M 2.2 m; F 2.3 m
LENGTH: 3.2 m (max.)
STATUS:
Vulnerable Globally (IUCN);
Secure in Australia

Zebra Shark *Stegostoma fasciatum*

Despite their name, Zebra Sharks are spotted, not striped, and should probably be called Leopard Sharks! Their most distinctive feature is a huge lobeless tail that is as long as the body. Zebra Sharks are bulky sharks with a blunt head, two long, low dorsal fins set well back on the body and two strong ridges that run along the upper body to the tail base.

DESCRIPTION: These sharks get their name from the colour pattern of small juveniles, which have alternating black and white zebra stripes. As they grow, these stripes break up to a pattern of dark spots on a yellow-brown body colour.

HABITAT: Zebra Sharks are usually seen resting on sandy bottoms close to coral reefs during the day.

BEHAVIOUR: Zebra Sharks probably hunt more actively at night. They can swim quite fast and are often seen swimming further above the bottom than other benthic (bottom-dwelling) sharks.

FEEDING HABITS: Zebra Sharks have many small, three-pointed teeth and feed mainly on molluscs that they dig from the sand. They will also eat crustaceans, worms and small fish.

BREEDING: These large sharks are oviparous. Females lay large egg cases that are dark brown and anchored by bunches of hair-like tendrils. The young are born at a length of about 20 cm.

DANGER TO HUMANS: Zebra Sharks can often be approached closely and are harmless to humans.

HABITAT & DISTRIBUTION: Zebra Sharks are found in shallow water around coral reefs throughout the Indo-Pacific and Red Sea

SEXUAL MATURITY: M & F 1.7 m

LENGTH: 2.4 m (max.)

STATUS: Vulnerable Globally (IUCN); Secure in Australia

Whale Shark *Rhincodon typus*

The Whale Shark is the largest living fish, but just how big these monstrous sharks grow has been subject to much debate. Recent measurements from satellite-tagged sharks and from the Taiwanese Whale Shark fishery have shown that they reach a maximum length of at least 18 m. Preliminary studies suggest these sharks may live for more than 100 years.

DESCRIPTION: Whale Sharks have broad heads and mouths, huge gill slits and a very high tail fin. They have a distinctive pattern of white stripes and spots on a brown body.

HABITAT: Whale Sharks are often seen swimming on the surface but studies have recently shown that they make regular dives to depths of 1 km.

BEHAVIOUR: Satellite tags have revealed that Whale Sharks make long migrations around the world and tend to associate in groups segregated by size and sex.

FEEDING HABITS: These huge sharks are plankton feeders, targeting food concentrations and gulping 10–20 large mouthfuls each minute, forcing the water out of their huge gill slits and swallowing the filtered food. They prefer copepods but also eat small fish and will seek out the eggs of mass spawning fish and corals.

BREEDING: Whale Sharks are ovoviviparous. One female was found with 300 young at three different stages of development — including some 50–60 cm long specimens on the verge of being born.

DANGER TO HUMANS: A harmless giant, divers often swim close to Whale Sharks in complete safety.

HABITAT & DISTRIBUTION:
Whale Sharks are pelagic sharks found far offshore or close to the coast through-out tropical and subtropical waters of the world

LENGTH:
12–18 m (max.)
WEIGHT:
36 t (max.)
STATUS:
Vulnerable (IUCN)

Along for the Ride

PILOTFISH

Many fish and other organisms live their lives associated with large predatory sharks — a lifestyle that seems at first glance to be very dangerous! Pilotfish (*Naucrates ductor*) are small trevallies with vivid black and silver vertical stripes, and they are often seen swimming right in front of a large shark's nose. These fish are riding the bow wave generated by the much larger shark and conserving swimming energy. Despite their name, Pilotfish do not guide sharks to their food, but they certainly take advantage of any scraps that remain after their large host has eaten. Juvenile Golden Trevally have a similar yellow and black striped pattern and a similar lifestyle. Both these small hitchhikers sometimes pick parasites from the shark's skin to supplement their diet. The contrasting stripes of these fish either

confuse the shark's vision or warn the sharks that these small hangers-on are helpful and are not to be eaten.

REMORAS

Remoras, or "shark suckers" as they are sometimes called, also accompany sharks for the scraps that result from their feeding activities. Rather than riding the sharks bow wave, these fish attach firmly to their hosts using a unique suction disc on top of their heads. The edge of this disc is pushed against the host's skin, and several slats across the disc contract to create suction and let the Remora ride along without effort.

Above: A lone Remora, showing the suction disc on top of its head that is used for attaching to larger hosts.

Forty years ago the Greynurse Shark had the reputation of being a dangerous "man-eater". This was based more on the shark's fierce, snaggletoothed appearance and large size rather than any confirmed attacks on swimmers or divers. Many of these amazing sharks were killed to "protect" swimmers before it was realised that this paranoia of attack was baseless.

DESCRIPTION: Greynurse Sharks are heavy-bodied with a pointed snout and two large equal-sized dorsal fins. Unlike most sharks, their dagger-like teeth are clearly displayed when swimming normally. These sharks have a pale belly and are bronze-coloured on the back with a scattering of dark spots that fade as they grow larger. Greynurse Sharks have an elongated upper tail lobe with a distinct notch near the end.

HABITAT: Greynurse Sharks are most often seen around coral or rocky reefs from southern NSW to southern Qld and in south-western WA.

BEHAVIOUR: These sharks are often seen in groups swimming slowly in sand-floored gutters during the day. Only about 25 such resting sites are known for the east coast population.

FEEDING HABITS: Greynurse Sharks feed mainly at night on bony fish and other sharks and rays. They often hunt in cooperative groups.

BREEDING: Females produce only two pups every second year. Young develop ovoviviparously, eating other young and unfertilised eggs.

DANGER TO HUMANS: These sharks have never made an unprovoked attack but they can deliver warning snaps and should be treated with care.

HABITAT & DISTRIBUTION: Bottom-living around rocky or coral reefs down to 200 m depth; found in warm temperate zones of all oceans

SEXUAL MATURITY:
M & F 2.2 m
LENGTH:
3.2 m (max.)
STATUS:
Vulnerable (IUCN)

Shark Teeth

DENTINE: Sharks and rays are colloquially called cartilaginous fish because they have a skeleton made out of relatively soft, light cartilage rather than heavy bone. Shark jaws are also made out of cartilage and are quite flexible and not solidly attached to the skull. Teeth made out of soft cartilage would be pretty useless, fortunately, shark teeth are made out of hard dentine like our own teeth.

CONTINUOUS REPLACEMENT: The teeth of sharks and rays are replaced continuously throughout their life on something like a "tooth conveyor belt". This allows teeth to increase in size as the shark grows and also ensures that broken, damaged or lost teeth are replaced quickly. Most sharks replace their teeth every 8–15 days, and there are usually at least five spare teeth of decreasing size waiting in line behind every main tooth. These are ready to swing up into use when a tooth is lost or broken.

MANY DIFFERENT TOOTH TYPES: Sharks and rays have many different tooth types, depending on their lifestyle and diet. Large predators have sharp cutting teeth that can be used to slice mouthfuls off big prey, but those that eat small slippery fish or squid often have long dagger-like gripping teeth. Bottom-grubbing sharks and rays often have flattened crushing teeth for breaking up hard-shelled prey items.

Top: Greynurse Shark teeth. **Above:** Greynurse Shark jaw, showing "conveyor belt" dentition.

The White Shark is the quintessential shark, the monster that sends shivers down everyone's spine. Its immense size, huge serrated teeth, fast movement and active, warm-blooded lifestyle make the White Shark the world's most feared ocean predator. White Shark blood circulation features a counter-current heat-exchange system to prevent losing heat (generated by muscle activity) through the skin. This keeps the shark's body temperature 5–14°C higher than the surrounding water.

DESCRIPTION: White Sharks have heavy bodies with sharp pointed snouts and large crescent-shaped tails that have almost equal-sized upper and lower lobes. This type of tail is described as homocercal (as opposed to the heterocercal tail of most sharks). The White Shark has five very long gill slits, a high pointed first dorsal fin and huge blue-black eyes. These sharks are blue-grey to grey-brown on the back and white on the belly, with a sharp demarcation along the side between the upper and lower colours.

HABITAT: White Sharks are most often seen in shallow coastal waters off southern Australia but also spend time in the open ocean far from shore. They often swim on the surface with their dorsal fin protruding from the water.

HABITAT & DISTRIBUTION: White Sharks live throughout most oceans, inshore to open sea, from the surface down to 1200 m

SEXUAL MATURITY: M 3.5–4.0 m; F 4.0–5.0 m

LENGTH: 6.1 m (max.)

WEIGHT: 2 t

STATUS: Vulnerable (IUCN)

BEHAVIOUR: These large sharks are usually solitary but may gather at preferred feeding sites (such as seal colonies) when conditions are right. Satellite tagging programs over the past five years have shed some light on White Shark behaviour. They are not territorial but make long migrations between feeding and breeding sites, stopping for weeks or months and then moving on again. Researchers were astounded when a tagged female recently made a 22,000 km journey from South Africa to Western Australia and back in about nine months. This shark made regular forays down to 1000 m depth and maintained an average speed of almost 5 km/h!

TEETH & FEEDING HABITS: White Sharks have 26 large triangular teeth in the upper jaw and 24 in the lower, all with sharp, serrated cutting edges. Young White Sharks feed mainly on fish, small sharks and rays. As they mature, many adults then change to a diet of marine mammals such as seals and dolphins, but some still subsist entirely on fish. White Sharks prefer food with a high fat content and will reject prey that taste tells them is not energy-rich.

BREEDING: These huge sharks take about 12–17 years to reach maturity and can live for up to 60 years. Mating has never been observed but probably takes place in special inshore breeding areas. Females give birth to 2–17 pups that eat other unfertilised eggs throughout their eighteen-month development. They are born at a length of about 1.3 m. Female White Sharks probably only give birth to about 80 pups during their fifty-year lifetime.

Opposite, top and bottom: The body features of a fast, open-ocean swimmer; A distensible jaw means large prey can be swallowed. **Above:** Swimming near the surface in glassy calm seas.

DANGER TO HUMANS: In terms of human fatalities, the White Shark is the most dangerous shark. There have been over 370 recorded attacks worldwide in the past 100 years, 63 of which have proved fatal. South Africa recorded 22 fatalities over an 83-year period. Around 40% of shark fatalities are caused by White Sharks. But to put these statistics into perspective, these sharks only cause about one fatality worldwide every two years.

WORLDWIDE DISTRIBUTION: White Sharks are found throughout most of the world's seas and oceans, ranging from the tropics to cold temperate waters 60° from the Equator. These sharks have been recorded from Alaska, the United Kingdom, northern Japan and Newfoundland in the Northern Hemisphere as well as near Cape Horn off southern South America. They are particularly abundant around southern Australia, New Zealand, South Africa and California. Although they prefer cool temperate waters and can deal with temperatures as low as 3°C for short periods, these sharks are also occasionally sighted in balmy tropic seas where the surface temperatures are over 30 °C.

CONSERVATION: Many White Sharks are caught in nets and on set lines, and over 670 have been caught in the Qld shark control program since 1962. White Sharks have been protected in South Africa since 1991 and are now protected in Australia and elsewhere. The Convention on the International Trade in Endangered Species (CITES) listed this shark as endangered in 2004.

Above: A White Shark excited by a cage diving operation. **Opposite, top to bottom:** White Sharks have large, widely spaced, serrated triangular teeth that are ideally suited for cutting up large prey; White Sharks often leap clear of the water while launching attacks on their prey.

Shortfin Mako *Isurus oxyrinchus*

The Shortfin Mako is the fastest shark in the world. These spectacular blue and white speedsters can swim at 60 km/h for short bursts and maintain speeds of 3–5 km/h on a long-distance migration. Makos often leap spectacularly to more than 5 m out of the water. Like the related White Sharks, makos maintain a body temperature up to 10 °C above that of the surrounding water.

DESCRIPTION: Like the White Shark, the Shortfin Mako is spindle-shaped with a sharp pointed snout, huge black eyes, large gill slits and a crescent-shaped tail. It has dagger-like teeth that show even when its mouth is closed (as does the Greynurse Shark). Shortfin Makos are bright blue on the back, silver-blue along the flanks and white on the belly. Larger individuals become more grey-blue, and very large makos may look like White Sharks.

HABITAT: Shortfin Makos live near the surface in the open ocean far from shore and are rarely seen except by offshore longliners. They do not like water colder than 16°C and will move closer to the Equator during winter months. These sharks do not normally venture deeper than about 150 m, preferring warmer surface waters.

BEHAVIOUR: Like other oceanic sharks, Shortfin Makos make long migrations. They regularly swim the span of the Tasman Sea between Australia and New Zealand. The longest recorded journey for a Shortfin Mako was over 4500 km.

HABITAT & DISTRIBUTION:
Pelagic sharks of the open ocean throughout temperate and tropical seas

SEXUAL MATURITY:
M 1.8 m; F 2.8 m

LENGTH: 4.0 m (max.)

WEIGHT: 500 kg

STATUS:
Near Threatened (IUCN)

FEEDING HABITS: These sharks are fast-swimming active predators on pelagic fish, squids and smaller sharks. Their dagger-like teeth are ideal for gripping small struggling prey, which is swallowed whole. They eat ten times their own body weight per year.

BREEDING: For reasons that are a mystery to humans, males mature at a much smaller size than females. After mating, females produce 4–16 young that feed on unfertilised eggs until they are born. At birth they are 60–70 cm.

DANGER TO HUMANS: Shortfin Mako Sharks only eat small fish and do not normally attack humans. There have been a few reports of these sharks biting swimmers but none of these assaults have been fatal.

Opposite, top and inset: The Shortfin Mako's body is built for speed; Makos have ragged-looking, dagger-like teeth ideal for gripping slippery prey. **Below:** Makos have a sharp pointed snout, large black eyes and very long gill slits.

Basking Shark Cetorhinus maximus

Basking Sharks are the world's second-largest fish and another gentle giant of the shark world. These huge filter-feeders have a gigantic wide-opening mouth, gill slits that almost meet around the head and a large homocercal tail. They have a long snout protruding like an afterthought over their huge maw.

DESCRIPTION: Non-feeding Basking Sharks swimming with their huge mouths closed have a strangely crumpled look around the mouth and head. This species is greyish-brown with a slightly paler belly.

HABITAT: Basking Sharks usually swim on the surface and prefer current convergence zones or upwelling areas where plankton swarm profusely.

BEHAVIOUR: Basking Sharks have huge oil-rich livers that help them to achieve almost neutral buoyancy. They are often found in groups and undertake long migrations, but little is known of their behaviour.

FEEDING HABITS: These sharks are "all mouth" and can open up like a huge plankton net to sieve small copepods and other small zooplankton from the water. They swim slowly while feeding, at about 3.5 km/h, and can filter about 2000 t of water per hour! Basking Sharks shed and regrow their gill rakers when plankton densities drop in the winter, but where they go and how they survive during this time is a mystery.

BREEDING: Basking Sharks are ovoviviparous and litters of six pups have been found in pregnant females. Pregnancies appear to last 2–3 years and these sharks probably live to more than 50 years of age.

DANGER TO HUMANS: Basking Sharks are harmless.

HABITAT & DISTRIBUTION: Basking Sharks frequent coastal and oceanic surface waters in all temperate regions

SEXUAL MATURITY: M 5–7 m; F 8 m
LENGTH: Approx. 10 m (max.)
WEIGHT: 7.5 t (max.)
STATUS: Vulnerable (IUCN); Protected in UK, NZ & USA

Opposite and above: A feeding Basking Shark opens its huge mouth to form an efficient plankton net that can filter about 2000 t of water every hour.

The Prickly Dogfish is a bizarre-looking, humpbacked shark with a triangular sectioned body and a pair of high, sail-like dorsal fins. These small deepwater sharks have a protective spine in front of each dorsal fin and, like all dogfish, they completely lack an anal fin. They have a high, weakly notched tail and a large breathing spiracle behind the eye with very short gill slits.

DESCRIPTION: The Prickly Dogfish derives its name from the large rough "scales" that cover its body. Shark scales (known as dermal denticles) are different from the scales of bony fish and resemble tiny teeth (see page 60). Prickly Dogfish are a uniform brown colour with white fin tips or margins.

HABITAT: Prickly Dogfish live on the continental slope sea floor.

BEHAVIOUR: Occasionally taken by trawlers targeting other fish species, the Prickly Dogfish is an elusive species. Nothing is known of this shark's behaviour, but the small gill slits suggest it is not very active. They are probably slow swimmers and may spend time resting on the bottom.

FEEDING HABITS: Prickly Dogfish have a small mouth with narrow, sharp gripping teeth in the upper jaw and a row of twelve blade-like teeth forming a jagged, serrated cutting edge in the lower jaw. They probably feed on invertebrates and small fish.

BREEDING: These sharks are ovoviviparous with a litter size of seven reported for one female.

DANGER TO HUMANS: Prickly Dogfish are considered harmless, but people should avoid this shark's fin spines.

HABITAT & DISTRIBUTION: Deepwater species, bottom-living on the outer shelf and slope from 50–650 m around southern Australia and New Zealand

SEXUAL MATURITY:
M & F approx. 60 cm

LENGTH:
72 cm (max.)

STATUS:
Data Deficient (IUCN)

The Brier Shark is a small deepwater shark with a long, flattened, spade-like snout and widely spaced nostrils. The whole body is flattened, about twice as wide as it is high, and the first dorsal fin is extremely long and low. Like all dogfish, there is a strong spine in front of each dorsal fin and no anal fin. The second dorsal fin spine is long and curved.

DESCRIPTION: These sharks have large, yellow eye pupils and are a uniform grey to dark brown. Young individuals have dark patches above the eye and gills and dark margins on their dorsal and tail fins.

HABITAT: Brier Sharks usually live on the continental slope sea floor.

BEHAVIOUR: Little is known of the behaviour of most deepwater sharks.

FEEDING HABITS: Brier Sharks have many awl-like teeth and feed on deepwater fish (such as hatchetfish and dragonfish) as well as deepwater prawns.

BREEDING: These sharks are ovoviviparous, but pregnant females are seldom caught in Australian waters. Litter sizes overseas range from 6–12 pups, which are born when they are about 30 cm long.

DANGER TO HUMANS: The Brier Shark is considered harmless. This shark is caught in large numbers overseas and utilised for its squalene-rich liver. Brier Sharks are also caught commonly in Australian waters but are not exploited here. Brier Sharks belong to the dogfish family, which is represented by more than 40 species in Australian waters.

HABITAT & DISTRIBUTION: Outer shelf and slope usually in 400–900 m; all temperate regions except for north America

SEXUAL MATURITY: M & F 70 cm
LENGTH: 1.1 m (max.)
STATUS: Secure

The Whiskery Shark is a houndshark that features distinctive long barbels near the front edge of each nostril beneath the chin. This shark has a long slender body with two widely separated, equal-sized dorsal fins and a breathing spiracle immediately behind the eye. A small anal fin is present immediately below the second dorsal fin.

DESCRIPTION: Whiskery Sharks are brown-grey on the back with a paler belly. Newborn young are cream coloured with irregular dark blotches on body and fins, but these blotches fade as the shark grows and may not be visible in large adults.

HABITAT: Most Whiskery Sharks are found on the continental shelf at depths of 50–90 m.

BEHAVIOUR: Little is known of this shark, and the nursery grounds where females give birth are unknown.

FEEDING HABITS: Whiskery Sharks feed mainly on cephalopods. They have a preference for octopuses but also eat small fish and crustaceans.

BREEDING: These sharks are ovoviviparous with litter sizes ranging from 5–24 pups, which are born when they are about 25 cm long after a 7–8 month pregnancy. Females give birth every two years and only live for 10–12 years. Lifetime offspring production corresponds to only 15–72 pups.

DANGER TO HUMANS: These harmless sharks are an important species in the Western Australian shark fishery and about 400 t were caught annually in the 1980s. This has since halved, but the catch is probably still not sustainable.

HABITAT & DISTRIBUTION:
Temperate continental shelf waters to 220 m depth between Northwest Cape and Bass Strait

SEXUAL MATURITY:
M & F 1.2 m
LENGTH:
1.6 m (max.)
STATUS:
Secure

School Sharks look like typical whaler sharks and were included in that family for many years, although they are now considered to be houndsharks like the Gummy Shark and Whiskery Shark. This species is a moderate-sized shark with a high first dorsal fin, an unusually small second dorsal and a small anal fin. The tail fin is large and the upper lobe is distinctly notched.

DESCRIPTION: School Sharks are bronze or grey-brown on the back and pale on the belly.

HABITAT: School Sharks usually swim near the bottom on the continental shelf but are sometimes seen by divers around rocky reefs.

BEHAVIOUR: A highly migratory species, School Sharks often travel in large single-sex schools and have discrete mating and nursery sites. Individuals have been recorded moving up to 1400 km in southern Australia.

FEEDING HABITS: School Sharks have sharp teeth and feed on fish and squid.

BREEDING: School Sharks are ovoviviparous and have large litters of 15–43 pups. They take 8–12 years to reach maturity and can live for at least 55 years.

DANGER TO HUMANS: Although they grow to a moderate size, School Sharks are not aggressive and have never been recorded as attacking a swimmer or diver. The School Shark is an important commercial species and has been heavily overfished. Because they are long-lived, School Sharks are vulnerable to fishing pressure and catch rates threaten to become unsustainable.

HABITAT & DISTRIBUTION: Near the seabed over the continental shelf and upper continental slope in temperate waters throughout much of the world

SEXUAL MATURITY: M 1.2 m; F 1.3 m

LENGTH: 1.75 m (max.)

STATUS: Vulnerable (IUCN)

Catshark Family

Catsharks form the largest shark family with over 100 species found worldwide. More than 30 of these are recorded from Australia. They are all small, thin sharks, usually 40–80 cm long as adults, with two similar-sized dorsal fins and long anal fins and tails. The name "catshark" comes from their small, elongate, cat-like eyes.

DESCRIPTION: Most deepwater species are uniform dark brown or black in colour but those that live on the continental shelf are pale with varied patterns of blotches, spots and stripes.

HABITAT: All catsharks are small bottom-living sharks. Some species are found as deep as 1500 m on the continental slope. Most Australian species are endemic.

BEHAVIOUR: Little is known of the behaviour of most catsharks but swellsharks in the genus *Cephaloscyllium* are able to blow themselves up like a balloon by swallowing water. This makes them look larger than they are and discourages predators that threaten them.

FEEDING HABITS: Catsharks have many small, three-pronged teeth in each jaw and feed on small fish, crustaceans and other invertebrates.

BREEDING: Catsharks lay eggs that are usually attached to the bottom by sticky tendrils until they hatch. The eggs of most species have not been found.

DANGER TO HUMANS: All species are small and harmless.

Blackspotted Catshark
Aulohalaelurus labiosus

SEXUAL MATURITY: M & F 55 cm

LENGTH: 67 cm (max.)

HABITAT & DISTRIBUTION: Restricted to shallow coastal and offshore reefs around south-western Australia

STATUS: Secure

Draughtboard Shark *Cephaloscyllium laticeps*

SEXUAL MATURITY: M & F 82 cm
LENGTH: 1.5 m (max.)
HABITAT & DISTRIBUTION:
Bottom-dwelling around reefs to
depths of 60 m across southern
Australia from Esperance to Jervis Bay
STATUS: Secure

Gulf Catshark *Asymbolus vincenti*

SEXUAL MATURITY: M & F 38 cm
LENGTH: 56 cm (max.)
HABITAT & DISTRIBUTION: Found on
the continental shelf down to 220 m
across southern Australia
STATUS: Secure

Grey Spotted Catshark *Asymbolus analis*

SEXUAL MATURITY: M & F 52 cm
LENGTH: 60 cm (max.)
HABITAT & DISTRIBUTION: Lives on
the bottom between 40 and 80 m
depth off the NSW coast
STATUS: Data Deficient (IUCN)

Most people who regularly dive on coral reefs have had frightening encounters with Grey Reef Sharks. These common reef sharks are sometimes eaten by Tiger and Bull Sharks and when threatened they display a cautionary arched-back. This warns they are fast and agile and will bite if the larger shark does not back off. Divers are often treated to the same display by these sharks.

DESCRIPTION: Grey Reef Sharks are moderate-sized, typical whaler sharks with a prominent black margin to the tail fin and black patches on the second dorsal, pelvic and underside tips of the pectoral fins. They are bronze grey on the back and pale on the belly.

HABITAT: Grey Reef Sharks are found in all coral reef habitats but are most abundant around passes and on steep drop-offs.

BEHAVIOUR: These sharks are very curious and often move in loose groups of up to a dozen individuals.

FEEDING HABITS: Grey Reef Sharks feed primarily on fish but also eat squids, octopuses and crustaceans.

BREEDING: These sharks are viviparous, like all whalers, and the developing young are fed through a yolk sac placenta. Females give birth to 2–4 pups every two years and only produce about fifteen offspring in their lifetime.

DANGER TO HUMANS: These sharks are only moderate-sized but if they feel threatened will occasionally give divers a quick warning bite.

HABITAT & DISTRIBUTION: Lives around coral reefs from the surface down to 280 m throughout the Indo–Pacific		SEXUAL MATURITY: M & F 1.35 m
		LENGTH: 2.55 m (max.); rare over 1.8 m
		STATUS: Near Threatened (IUCN)

Silky Shark *Carcharhinus falciformis*

The Silky Shark is an oceanic species that is seldom seen by any humans except offshore purse seine fishers. Silky Sharks have a typical whaler shark shape but with the first dorsal fin positioned well behind the rear edge of the pectoral fins. The Silky Shark's second dorsal and anal fins are small and set back near the tail (as in all whaler sharks), but these fins also feature distinctive, long, rear trailing edges.

DESCRIPTION: These sharks are a uniform dark grey on the back and white on the belly. They get their name from the silky smooth feel of their skin.

HABITAT: Silky Sharks are most abundant near the surface along the outer edge of the continental shelf.

BEHAVIOUR: Silky Sharks are fast-moving and active. They boldly approach divers and may act quite aggressively.

FEEDING HABITS: Silky Sharks often follow tuna schools and eat tuna and other fish as well as the occasional squid, paper nautilus or pelagic crab.

BREEDING: Silky Sharks are viviparous and females give birth to about 2–15 pups that are 70–85 cm long. The nursery area for their young sharks is usually a little closer to the coast than the normal adult habitat.

DANGER TO HUMANS: Although Silky Sharks are aggressive they have never been recorded as attacking humans.

HABITAT & DISTRIBUTION:
A pelagic shark that lives worldwide in tropical offshore waters down to depths of 500 m

SEXUAL MATURITY:
M & F 2–2.1 m
LENGTH:
3.3 m (max.)
STATUS:
Secure

Blue Shark *Prionace glauca*

Blue Sharks are the most abundant sharks in the world's oceans. It is estimated that over five million Blue Sharks are caught each year as bycatch in the offshore tuna longline fishery. They are also one of the most beautiful sharks, with a graceful shape and long curving pectoral fins. Their first dorsal fin is relatively low but the tail fin, like the pectoral fins, is large and long.

DESCRIPTION: As their name suggests, Blue Sharks are a bright indigo blue on the back with silver-blue flanks and a pure white belly.

HABITAT: Blue Sharks are an offshore, pelagic species that hunt in the surface waters of open oceans. They prefer water temperatures between 12–20°C and often move into deeper water in the tropics.

BEHAVIOUR: Food is scarce in the open ocean and Blue Sharks have adopted a low-energy lifestyle to get by on slim pickings. They normally swim slowly and appear to be quite sluggish. These sharks migrate long distances and move closer to the equator in winter.

HABITAT & DISTRIBUTION:
Blue Sharks are abundant in all the world's offshore seas from the surface down to about 350 m depth

SEXUAL MATURITY:
M & F 2.2 m
LENGTH:
3.8 m (max.)
STATUS:
Near Threatened (IUCN)

FEEDING HABITS: Blue Sharks feed on squids and small fish and often gather in large numbers around spawning aggregations of pelagic squid. They eat most oceanic fish species (including sardines, flying fish and small tuna) as well as a range of invertebrates such as pelagic crabs, shrimps and octopuses.

BREEDING: Blue Sharks display highly vigorous courtship behaviour during which males bite females on their flanks and fins. To cope with such attention, females have skin up to three times as thick as the males.

These sharks have larger litters than any other shark, with an average of about 40 pups. The maximum number recorded was an incredible 135 young. Blue Sharks grow rapidly and reach maturity in only 4–6 years.

DANGER TO HUMANS: Blue Sharks can be aggressive and have bitten divers on a few occasions, but no fatalities have been reported.

Opposite, top and bottom: Valerie Taylor tries out a steel mesh suit for protection from the bites of an excited Blue Shark. **Below:** Blue Shark cruising in its ocean realm.

Oceanic Whitetip Shark

Carcharhinus longimanus

The Oceanic Whitetip Shark is a large offshore pelagic species like the Blue Shark. They are seldom seen by divers but are very easy to identify when they are encountered. These sharks are very solidly built, and as adults have very large, rounded fins with irregular or mottled white tips.

DESCRIPTION: Oceanic Whitetips are bronze-grey on the back with a paler belly. Newborn young have black tips on most fins but these fade when the shark grows to about 1.3 m long and the distinctive mottled white tips develop on the first dorsal, pectoral, pelvic and tail fins.

HABITAT: These sharks live near the surface in offshore oceanic waters where the temperature is over 20°C.

BEHAVIOUR: Oceanic Whitetip Sharks are slow-moving but can be persistently aggressive around possible sources of food. A dead whale may attract loose feeding aggregations of these sharks. Oceanic Whitetips migrate to avoid cold water.

FEEDING HABITS: A wide variety of pelagic fish and cephalopods are eaten, as well as large prey animals.

BREEDING: Oceanic Whitetips are viviparous and females have litters of 1–15 pups after a pregnancy of about twelve months.

DANGER TO HUMANS: These sharks are regarded as one of the world's four most dangerous species of shark (along with the White, Tiger and Bull Sharks). These sharks exacted a heavy death toll following offshore ship disasters during World War I and II.

HABITAT & DISTRIBUTION:
An oceanic pelagic shark found worldwide in tropical waters down to depths of 150 m

SEXUAL MATURITY:
M & F 1.8–2 m
LENGTH:
3.5 m (max.)
STATUS:
Vulnerable (IUCN)

Above: An Oceanic Whitetip cruises in the open ocean surrounded by Pilotfish.

The Whitetip Reef Shark is the most abundant of the coral reef sharks and several are usually seen on most coral reef dives around tropical Australia. These elongate whaler shark relatives have a small blunt head and distinct white tips on the first dorsal and upper tail lobe. Both dorsal fins are high and pointed, with the second about two-thirds the height of the first.

DESCRIPTION: These moderate-sized sharks are grey-brown on the back, usually with a few darker spots. They are white on the belly.

HABITAT: Whitetip Reef Sharks are bottom-living on coral reefs. They are most abundant in the upper 50 m but have been recorded as deep as 300 m.

BEHAVIOUR: Whitetip Reef Sharks usually swim slowly just above the seabed and spend a lot of time resting on the bottom in sandy-floored caves and overhangs. They hunt and feed both day and night and are usually solitary, unless attracted to a bait.

FEEDING HABITS: Whitetips hunt the reef and sea floor for small fish, crustaceans and octopuses.

BREEDING: Whitetip Reef Sharks are one of the few sharks that have been observed mating. The couple were resting parallel to each other, head-down on the bottom. These sharks mature at eight years of age and females give birth to only two pups every second year. Whitetip Reef Sharks live about twenty years and each female only has about twelve young during her entire life.

DANGER TO HUMANS: Whitetips are not normally aggressive or dangerous but divers that handle or annoy them are sometimes bitten.

HABITAT & DISTRIBUTION:
These sharks live on coral reefs throughout the Indo–Pacific down to depths of about 50 m

SEXUAL MATURITY:
M & F 1.05 m

LENGTH:
1.7 m (max.)

STATUS:
Near Threatened (IUCN)

Above, top to bottom: Whitetip Reef Sharks often rest on the bottom; These sharks usually swim just above the sea floor.

Bull Shark *Carcharhinus leucas*

Although it is not as notorious as the White Shark in Australia, the Bull Shark is one of the most dangerous sharks. These solid-bodied whaler sharks live in coastal waters where most people swim and play, so they often come into contact with humans. They are sometimes called "river whalers" because they may travel far up rivers and can even breed in completely fresh water.

DESCRIPTION: Bull Sharks are dark grey on the back and pale on the belly. They are a large shark with a blunt round head and a high, sharply pointed first dorsal fin.

The hind edge of the first dorsal fin is almost vertical and the second dorsal fin is more than a third as high as the first. They are a long-lived species.

HABITAT: Bull Sharks are specialised for life in inshore, dirty water, but they are also found around offshore coral reefs down to depths of about 150 m. Young Bull Sharks are common in tropical rivers around northern Australia and may occasionally be seen leaping completely clear of the water.

BEHAVIOUR: These sharks are usually solitary and are large and aggressive.

FEEDING HABITS: Bull Sharks will eat almost anything, large or small, that is edible. Their diet includes fish, other sharks, turtles, dolphins, crustaceans, squids, molluscs and echinoderms.

HABITAT & DISTRIBUTION:
Lives in coastal waters, estuaries and rivers throughout tropical and subtropical regions worldwide

SEXUAL MATURITY:
M 1.6–2. m; F 1.8–2.3 m
LENGTH:
3.4 m (max.)
STATUS:
Near Threatened (IUCN)

BREEDING: Bull Sharks have litters of 1–13 pups that are born after an eleven-month pregnancy. They take about six years to reach maturity and live for at least fifteen years.

DANGER TO HUMANS: Although Bull Sharks are usually ranked behind White and Tiger Sharks in the danger stakes, they live in places heavily populated by people and are probably a more dangerous species. Many of the early shark attacks on northern Australian beaches prior to the instigation of the shark netting program were probably attributable to Bull Sharks. There have been several recent attacks by 2.5-3.0 m Bull Sharks on spearfishers around coral reefs off the north-east coast of Australia.

Above: Bull Sharks are bulky animals with a blunt rounded head and a sharp pointed first dorsal fin.

Small Blacktip Reef Sharks are one of the more common coral reef sharks and are often seen hunting over shallow reef flats with dorsal fin and tail tip showing. They are a small whaler shark with a distinctive black tip on their first dorsal fin that is often made more prominent by having a pale band beneath it.

DESCRIPTION: These sharks are pale yellow-brown on the back and white on the belly, with the distinctive black dorsal tip that gives them their name and another large black tip on their lower tail fin lobe.

HABITAT: Blacktip Reef Sharks are most abundant on shallow reef flats and in lagoons and are rarely seen at depths greater than about 10 m.

BEHAVIOUR: These sharks often gather in loose groups and are quick to investigate any disturbance.

FEEDING HABITS: Fish are a major part of the Blacktip Reef Shark's diet, but they also eat squids, crustaceans and molluscs. Interestingly, coastal populations have been found to eat lots of terrestrial snakes.

BREEDING: Like all whalers, Blacktip Reef Sharks are viviparous and produce 3–4 pups every one or two years.

DANGER TO HUMANS: Blacktip Reef Sharks usually flee from divers or snorkellers but they occasionally bite the legs or feet of people wading on reef flats.

Top: There is a paler band beneath the black marking on the dorsal fin. **Opposite, top to bottom:** Blacktip Reef Sharks have distinctive, sharply delineated black tips on the tail, first dorsal and underside of their pectoral fins.

HABITAT & DISTRIBUTION:
In shallow water around coral reefs throughout the tropical Indo–Pacific

SEXUAL MATURITY:
M & F 95–110 cm
LENGTH:
1.4 m (max.)
STATUS:
Near Threatened (IUCN)

Dusky Whaler *Carcharhinus obscurus*

Dusky Whalers belong to a group of large dark whalers lacking obvious fin markings, making them hard to identify without detailed examination. This group includes the Bull Shark, Pigeye Shark, Bronze Whaler, Silky Shark and Galapagos Shark. Only small details of fin shape and proportion, and tooth shape, separate these sharks, although their behaviour and lifestyles often differ considerably.

DESCRIPTION: The Dusky Whaler is grey on the back and pale beneath, with faint dusky tips on many of the fins — these are more pronounced in young sharks. They have a concave hind margin to the pectoral fins.

HABITAT: Dusky Whalers do not often visit reefs and are seldom seen by divers. They are common over the continental shelf and appear to migrate north and into deeper water as they age. Adults are most abundant in subtropical waters but also occur throughout Australia's northern tropics.

BEHAVIOUR: In Western Australia there is a Dusky Whaler nursery area in inshore waters between Albany and Lancelin. Adults make seasonal migrations to keep in preferred water temperatures.

FEEDING HABITS: Dusky Whalers mainly eat fish and smaller sharks but also feed on cephalopods (such as squids and octopuses) as well as crustaceans.

BREEDING: Dusky Whalers grow very slowly and take more than 20 years to reach maturity, with a life expectancy of more than 40 years. Females are viviparous and produce 3–14 pups every two to three years that are 70–100 cm long at birth.

HABITAT & DISTRIBUTION:
In mid-water over the shelf and upper slope to 400 m throughout tropical and temperate regions of the world

SEXUAL MATURITY:
M & F 2.8 m
LENGTH:
3.65 m (max.)
STATUS:
Near Threatened (IUCN)

DANGER TO HUMANS: These large sharks are potentially dangerous, but very few attacks have ever been reported and no fatalities are attributed to this species. Dusky Whalers are heavily fished in WA with peak catches of around 600 t annually in the 1980s. This fishery mainly targets near-newborn sharks from the nursery area (for the fish and chip trade) but declining annual catches (300 t in 2004) has shifted exploitation onto Gummy and Sandbar Sharks. These Dusky Whaler populations are seriously overfished and new restrictions are being applied to the fishery to try to save them. The long-term sustainable catch of a large, long-lived shark that produces low numbers of offspring is very low, and even incidental recreational catches can seriously reduce population numbers.

Many of the large whaler sharks found around Australia are known as "bronzies" but the true Bronze Whaler is found in shallow water only around southern Australia between Jurien Bay and Coffs Harbour. There are no obvious external features to separate the Bronze Whaler from other large dark whalers except a rounded first dorsal fin tip and the fact that the front of the first dorsal fin is level with the hind edge of the pectoral fins.

DESCRIPTION: These sharks are usually bronze to grey on the back but their colour is not strongly different from many other whalers. They usually have no obvious fin markings.

HABITAT: Bronze Whalers are often seen by divers around rocky reefs throughout southern Australia. They also often patrol in small to large schools just outside the surf zone during summer.

BEHAVIOUR: These sharks may act aggressively towards spearfishers when excited by the sound and smell of speared fish.

FEEDING HABITS: Bronze Whalers feed on fish and cephalopods and often gather in groups to hunt cooperatively for schooling fish such as Australian Salmon. They often migrate to follow preferred prey species.

BREEDING: Females give birth every two years to 10–20 young, which are born when they are 60–70 cm long.

DANGER TO HUMANS: Like all large whalers, Bronze Whalers are potentially dangerous to humans and have sometimes bitten divers and swimmers, but they have not been responsible for any verified fatalities.

HABITAT & DISTRIBUTION:
Bronze Whalers live around rocky reefs and over sand bottoms down to 100 m in temperate waters through-out the world

SEXUAL MATURITY:
M & F 2.4 m
LENGTH:
3.0 m (max.)
STATUS:
Near Threatened (IUCN)

Above: A group of large Bronze Whalers patrolling in shallow water outside the surf zone on the east Australian coast.

Tiger Sharks are the tropical equivalent of the White Shark and these large and dangerous predators have caused many fatalities over the past century. The largest Tiger Shark reliably measured was about the same size as the largest White Shark and Great Hammerhead (6 m), but 7 m long giants have been reported and they are possibly the largest of all predatory sharks.

DESCRIPTION: With a huge blunt head, and dark tiger stripes on a grey body above a white belly, these sharks are unmistakeable. The eyes are large and dark and the long, pointed upper tail lobe lacks a distinct notch.

HABITAT: This species lives in most habitats, from estuaries and rivers to the open ocean, and from shallow reef flats to deep reef slopes.

BEHAVIOUR: The usually solitary Tiger Shark is a great traveller, making journeys of hundreds or thousands of kilometres, but these migrations are not regular, and do not follow set routes.

Top: A mature Tiger Shark showing the distinct stripes that give this species its common name.
Above: Close-up of a Tiger Shark's dermal denticles.

HABITAT & DISTRIBUTION: Around reefs and in open water to depths of 150 m in tropical and subtropical seas worldwide

SEXUAL MATURITY: M 3 m; F 3.3 m

LENGTH: 6 m (max.)

STATUS: Near Threatened (IUCN)

Tiger Sharks may make long open ocean voyages where they venture far from land, but they also commonly cruise in shallow coastal waters and often enter estuaries and large rivers. They usually move up into shallow water at night and hunt actively around reef areas, but descend into deeper water during the day and swim more slowly than they do at night.

FEEDING HABITS: Tiger Sharks will eat anything — whether edible or inedible. They have wide cutting teeth with sharp, obliquely slanted tips and can easily slice up the shell of a fully grown marine turtle. They eat fish, other sharks and rays, crustaceans, sea snakes, birds, octopuses and squids. Tiger Sharks are more active and aggressive at night but also feed during the day.

BREEDING: Female Tiger Sharks are viviparous and give birth to 10–80 pups every two years.

DANGER TO HUMANS: Tiger Sharks frequent habitats where humans commonly swim and dive and have been responsible for more attacks than any other species except the White Shark. Shark netting has reduced their numbers inshore but they are still common in offshore waters.

The Lemon Shark is a large whaler shark that is unusually easy to identify because both high pointed dorsal fins are similarly sized. The anal and pelvic fins are also high and pointed and these sharks have a short blunt snout. This combination of features easily distinguishes them from all other large whalers.

DESCRIPTION: As their name suggests, Lemon Sharks are pale yellow-brown on the back with a pale belly. They have no fin markings.

HABITAT: Lemon Sharks are frequently seen swimming in water barely deep enough to float them — among mangroves, off beaches and on reef flats. Young sharks are often seen in loose schools and are very site-attached.

BEHAVIOUR: Young Lemon Sharks are curious and will investigate divers and swimmers but adults are normally shy. These sharks are more active at night than during the day.

FEEDING HABITS: Lemon Sharks have sharp, dagger-like teeth and feed on bottom-living fish and rays.

BREEDING: Females are viviparous and give birth to litters of 1–14 pups after a 10–11 month pregnancy. Newborn sharks are 50–70 cm long.

DANGER TO HUMANS: Despite the relative shyness of adults, Lemon Sharks become very aggressive if touched, speared or provoked. This species has bitten divers overseas. Although they are occasionally seen around coral reefs in tropical water, there have been no recorded Lemon Shark attacks in Australia.

HABITAT & DISTRIBUTION:
Inshore waters around reefs and beaches to depths of 30 m throughout the tropical Indo–Pacific

SEXUAL MATURITY:
M & F 2.2 m
LENGTH: 3 m (max.)
STATUS: Vulnerable (IUCN);
Secure in Australia;
Endangered in South-East Asia

Galapagos Sharks are seldom seen but are very common in their preferred habitat of isolated oceanic reefs. Around Australia they are only found around Lord Howe Island and on nearby Elizabeth and Middleton Reefs. Galapagos Sharks look very similar to Grey Reef Sharks, and seem to take the place of these sharks where they occur, but do not have the wide black margin on the tail fin of Grey Reef Sharks.

DESCRIPTION: The Galapagos Shark is a typical graceful whaler shark with a grey back and white belly. It has dusky tips on all fins except the first dorsal. Although they appear similar, the black on the Galapagos tail fin is not as pronounced as for the Grey Reef Shark.

HABITAT: These sharks live only on isolated oceanic coral reefs down to depths of about 180 m.

BEHAVIOUR: Adult Galapagos Sharks move into deeper water than the young and are seldom seen by divers. Immature Galapagos Sharks often gather in large groups that may have from ten to more than 100 individuals.

FEEDING HABITS: These sharks feed mainly on reef fish but also catch flying fish, squids and octopuses.

BREEDING: Litter size for the Galapagos Shark ranges from 6–16 pups that are born when they are 60–80 cm long.

DANGER TO HUMANS: Schools of young Galapagos Sharks can be very curious and intimidating to divers but are seldom dangerous. Large adults are more aggressive and should be treated with caution. Several attacks on swimmers and divers have been reported overseas, but only one of these attacks has proved fatal.

HABITAT & DISTRIBUTION: Galapagos Sharks live around isolated oceanic reefs and islands in the tropics and subtropics worldwide

SEXUAL MATURITY: M 2.2 m; F 2.5 m

LENGTH: 3 m (max.)

STATUS: Near Threatened Globally (IUCN); Data Deficient in Australia

The Pigeye Shark, or Black Whaler as it is sometimes known, looks almost identical to the Bull Shark and has the same sharp pointed first dorsal fin with a vertical hind edge. The only distinguishing feature between these species is the relative height of the second dorsal fin. In Pigeye Sharks this fin is small and less than a third the size of the first dorsal whereas in Bull Sharks it is larger — more than a third the size of the first.

DESCRIPTION: Like the Bull Shark, this species is a large, bulky shark with a short blunt snout. The Pigeye Shark is grey on the back and pale beneath, with no obvious fin markings as adults.

HABITAT: Pigeye Sharks live in shallow water around reefs and over the continental shelf.

BEHAVIOUR: Young Pigeye Sharks do not move far; however, tagged adults have been found to migrate more than 1000 km.

FEEDING HABITS: Bottom-living fish make up the bulk of this shark's diet, but it also eat sharks and rays, cephalopods and crustaceans.

BREEDING: Female Pigeye Sharks probably only breed every two years and give birth to 6–13 pups that are 60–65 cm long.

DANGER TO HUMANS: Unlike the very similar Bull Shark, this species has never been reliably implicated in an attack on a human. Divers occasionally see Pigeye Sharks around offshore coral reefs, where they sometimes make close approaches. They may behave aggressively and, because of physical similarities with the Bull Shark, it is possible that some offshore attacks attributed to Bull Sharks were actually perpetrated by the Pigeye Shark.

HABITAT & DISTRIBUTION:
Lives around coastal reefs down to about 100 m in the tropical and subtropical Indo–Pacific

SEXUAL MATURITY:
M 2.1 m; F 2.15 m
LENGTH:
2.8 m (max.)
STATUS:
Data Deficient (IUCN)

The Sandbar Shark is a moderate-sized whaler shark that has no diagnostic fin markings but is easy to identify by the extreme height of its first dorsal fin. This sail-like fin is positioned well forward on the back and overlaps about half the width of the pectoral fins. It is proportionally much higher than in any other whaler and is about as high as the length of the head.

DESCRIPTION: Sandbar Sharks are pale bronze or grey-brown on the back and pale on the belly.

HABITAT: These sharks live near the bottom from close inshore across the continental shelf to the upper slope.

BEHAVIOUR: Like most shark species, Sandbar Shark juveniles live in nursery areas separate from adults. In the North Atlantic, adults make seasonal migrations of thousands of kilometres so they are always living in warm waters. In Australia, however, this species' behaviour is not well-known.

FEEDING HABITS: Sandbar Sharks feed mainly on bottom-living fish but also eat squids and crustaceans.

BREEDING: These sharks are slow-growing and long-lived, taking 10–15 years to reach maturity and living for 30–50 years. Females give birth to an average of six pups every two years.

DANGER TO HUMANS: These harmless sharks are caught commercially and about 300 t of them are killed annually off Western Australia. These catches are unsustainable and populations of this distinctive large whaler shark have been depleted throughout much of its range.

HABITAT & DISTRIBUTION:
Bottom-dwelling over the continental shelf and upper slope to 280 m in tropical and temperate seas worldwide

SEXUAL MATURITY:
M & F 1.55 m

LENGTH:
2.4 m (max.)

STATUS:
Near Threatened (IUCN)

Great Hammerheads are impressive animals and one of the largest predatory sharks. At 6 m long they rival the White and Tiger Sharks but are not as heavy-bodied. Like all hammerheads, they have flattened wing-like extensions on each side of the head with their eyes and nostrils located at their tips. There has been much debate about the purpose of this strange head shape.

DESCRIPTION: The front edge of the hammer of the Great Hammerhead is almost straight, whereas in other hammerheads it is swept back. These sharks have relatively small pectoral fins but an enormous, sickle-shaped first dorsal that is over a metre high in a large adult. The upper tail lobe of a large Great Hammerhead may be as long as an average human adult.

HABITAT: Great Hammerheads often swim in very shallow water with the dorsal fin and tail tip showing.

BEHAVIOUR: Few details are known about the behaviour of these sharks.

FEEDING HABITS: Great Hammerheads feed on the bottom and eat a lot of stingrays and smaller sharks, as well as bony fish, cephalopods and crustaceans. A Great Hammerhead was once caught that had 96 broken stingray barbs embedded in its head!

BREEDING: Great Hammerheads are viviparous and produce large litters of 13–42 pups.

DANGER TO HUMANS: Despite their large size, Great Hammerheads usually ignore swimmers and divers except when they are excited by fish-feeding or spearfishing activities. They have been responsible for a few attacks over the years but no fatalities have resulted.

HABITAT & DISTRIBUTION:
Coastal waters in tropical and subtropical seas worldwide, around reefs and sandy bottoms to depths of 80 m

SEXUAL MATURITY:
M 2.3–2.7 m; F 2.5–3 m

LENGTH:
6 m (max.)

STATUS: Endangered (IUCN);
Data Deficient in Australia

*The Scalloped Hammerhead has swept-back head lobes and a straight, rather than sickle-shaped, high first dorsal fin. This species gets its name from the distinct notch in the centre of the front of the hammer; the very similar Smooth Hammerhead (*Sphyrna zygaena*) of temperate waters lacks this notch. Recent genetic studies have shown that the Atlantic population of the Scalloped Hammerhead is an almost identical, but separate, species.*

DESCRIPTION: The second dorsal, pelvic and anal fins of Scalloped Hammerheads are smaller than the same fins of Great Hammerheads.

HABITAT: These sharks are often seen in shallow water around coral reefs but adult females apparently live in deep water and only come onto the shelf to mate or give birth.

BEHAVIOUR: Scalloped Hammerheads often form large schools of more than 500 individuals. Much social interaction takes place in these schools but the reason for these amazing gatherings is still a mystery.

FEEDING HABITS: Like most sharks, Scalloped Hammerheads will feed during the day but are more active at night. They feed mainly on pelagic bony fish and cephalopods.

BREEDING: These viviparous sharks have litters of 13–23 pups that are born between October and January after a pregnancy of 9–10 months. Females move into shallow water to give birth.

DANGER TO HUMANS: Scalloped Hammerheads are usually timid but may become excited when fish are speared. Whether this species is responsible for any attacks is unknown.

HABITAT & DISTRIBUTION:
Lives over the continental shelf and upper slope to 275 m in tropical and warm temperate regions worldwide

SEXUAL MATURITY:
M 1.5 m; F 2 m
LENGTH:
3.5 m (max.)
STATUS:
Near Threatened (IUCN)

Angelsharks look like a cross between a shark and a ray, but are deemed to be sharks because their gill slits are on the side of the head, rather than underneath. These sharks have greatly enlarged and flattened pectoral and pelvic fins like a ray, but a normal shark-like hind body with two equal-sized dorsal fins. Angelsharks swim using to-and-fro tail movements.

DESCRIPTION: Australian Angelsharks are mottled pale grey-brown on the back with a scattering of white spots and a few irregular dark spots. Fin edges are often pale and the underside is white. These sharks have a pair of large multi-fringed barbels beneath the chin.

HABITAT: Australian Angelsharks are most abundant on shallow water sea floors through Bass Strait or off surf beaches around south-east Australia.

BEHAVIOUR: These sharks spend daylight hours resting — well camouflaged and partially buried — on the sandy bottom.

FEEDING HABITS: Angelsharks have many small sharp teeth in both jaws. They are probably lurking predators that erupt from the sand to eat small fish, squids, crabs or shrimps.

BREEDING: Females release unfertilised eggs into their two uteruses to feed developing young so these sharks are ovoviviparous. Litter size is up to seven pups that are about 30 cm long at birth.

DANGER TO HUMANS: Australian Angelsharks are not aggressive but have bitten divers who molested them. Angelshark flesh has an excellent taste and these sharks are commercially caught and sold as "flake" in Melbourne and Sydney.

HABITAT & DISTRIBUTION:
Lives on the coastal continental shelf down to 130 m over sandy bottoms around southern Australia

SEXUAL MATURITY:
M & F 60–70 cm

LENGTH:
1.5 m (max.)

STATUS:
Secure

Common Sawshark *Pristiophorus cirratus*

Sawsharks are curious-looking creatures. They have a relatively normal shark-like body but have a long flattened bony snout with sharp teeth down each side — much like that of the ray-related sawfish. This saw is about half the length of the sawshark's body. There is a pair of long sensory feelers (barbels) that stick out halfway along each side of the saw like a moustache.

DESCRIPTION: Common Sawsharks have two equal-sized dorsal fins and large eyes. They are pale yellowish or reddish brown on the back with darker bands, blotches and spots. The saw is pinkish with dark bands.

HABITAT: These sharks live on the bottom on the outer continental shelf and upper slope between Eden in southern New South Wales and Jurien Bay in Western Australia.

BEHAVIOUR: Common Sawsharks are sometimes found in schools but little is known about the behaviour of this deepwater species.

FEEDING HABITS: The Common Sawshark's sensory feelers are used to find prey hidden in the sand, which is then dug up with the saw and impaled with a sideways swipe. Common Sawsharks eat crabs, shrimps, small fish and other sand-living animals.

BREEDING: Common Sawsharks are ovoviviparous and give birth to 7–17 young that are about 40 cm long at birth. The developing embryo's teeth lie flat against the saw until birth to protect the mother!

DANGER TO HUMANS: Common Sawsharks are not aggressive but the saw may cause injuries if they are caught and handled.

HABITAT & DISTRIBUTION:
On soft substratum sea floors from 40–300 m depth around southern Australia

SEXUAL MATURITY: M & F 1 m
LENGTH: 1.3 m (max.)
STATUS: Secure

Rays

Rays are shark relatives that have adapted to life on the sea bottom. Their bodies have become flattened and the pectoral fins have become greatly expanded to form the diamond-shaped or circular body plan characteristic of most rays. Their gill slits have moved to the underside of the body and it is this configuration that forms the main distinction between sharks and rays. Some rays have become more mobile, elongated and shark-like, but if the gill slits are underneath they are still regarded as rays. Rays have eyes on the top of their body disc but the mouth, nostrils and gill slits lie underneath. Because rays rest flat on the bottom they cannot take in water through the mouth to pass over their gills (as most sharks do), so they have developed a large breathing spiracle behind the eye. Water is sucked into the spiracle, a one-way valve is closed and the water is then forced over the gills and out the gill slits. Most rays swim by undulating or flapping their "wings" rather than with side-to-side movements of the tail. The tail of most rays has become thin and even whip-like and usually bears a protective spine — the sting that gives stingrays their name. This dagger-like spine has a serrated edge and ranges in length from 10–30 cm. It can be wielded with great force to discourage attacks by large sharks — the major predators of rays.

Left: The tail spine or sting of all stingrays has a venom gland at its base and can cause severe wounds. **Opposite:** Large stingrays often move into shallow water when hunting for molluscs and other invertebrates that form a large part of their diet.

The Green Sawfish is a huge animal that can grow to over 7 m long. Its name refers to the long, flat bony rostrum or "saw" that extends from the tip of the snout and has a row of strong sharp teeth down each side. The hind body is shark-like, with two large, equal-sized dorsal fins, but the front of the body is flattened and has large triangular pectoral fins.

DESCRIPTION: As its name suggests, the Green Sawfish has a distinctly greenish-brown back. Its belly is white.

HABITAT: These sawfish live mainly on sand or mud bottoms in dirty coastal waters, or in estuaries and river mouths.

BEHAVIOUR: The Green Sawfish swims like a shark rather than with flaps or undulations of its large pectoral fins.

FEEDING HABITS: The Green Sawfish's formidable saw is slashed sideways to stun or impale prey, which is then wiped off against the bottom and picked up with the sawfish's small flattened teeth. Green Sawfish feed on fish, crabs and shrimps.

BREEDING: Sawfish are ovoviviparous and do not mature until they are over 4 m long. Embryo sawfish have a flexible saw and relatively soft teeth so they don't damage their mother before they are born.

DANGER TO HUMANS: These huge sawfish are not normally aggressive toward humans but if they are trapped in a net or cornered they can cause serious injuries with their saw. Many sawfish are caught accidentally in commercial inshore netting operations throughout northern Australia, and their numbers have been markedly reduced in recent decades.

HABITAT & DISTRIBUTION:
Lives in shallow coastal water and estuaries throughout the tropical Indo–West Pacific

SEXUAL MATURITY:
M & F 4.3 m

LENGTH:
7.3 m (max.)

STATUS:
Critically Endangered (IUCN)

Opposite and above: The large, toothed nose saw of a Green Sawfish is primarily used to capture or disable prey, but it also makes a lethal defensive weapon.

Southern Fiddler Ray   *Trygonorrhina fasciata*

Fiddler rays are named because of their supposed resemblance to the musical instrument. The front half of their body is flattened and ray-like but their hind body and tail looks like an elongate shark's. These rays use undulations of their pectoral fins when browsing on the bottom but utilise the tail when rapid swimming is required.

DESCRIPTION: Southern Fiddler Rays do not have the protective tail spine of a normal ray but instead have a line of small thorns down the centre of the back. They are yellow-brown on the back, with a pattern of bright blue-and-white lines, and white beneath. The markings are darker and brighter blue in young individuals.

HABITAT: Fiddler rays live on sandy bottoms in shallow water. A very similar species is found off the southern Queensland and New South Wales coasts.

BEHAVIOUR: Fiddler rays spend a lot of time resting on the bottom and are probably more active at night.

FEEDING HABITS: Southern Fiddler Rays have small blunt teeth fused into crushing plates. They feed on crabs and shrimps and other invertebrates as well as small fish. These rays will scavenge whenever opportunities arise, and often enter cray traps.

BREEDING: Female Southern Fiddler Rays produce golden egg cases that enclose 2–3 developing young. These cases are held in the mother's uteruses until the pups hatch.

DANGER TO HUMANS: These small spineless rays are harmless.

HABITAT & DISTRIBUTION:
Bottom-dwelling in shallow water across southern Australia

SEXUAL MATURITY:
Unknown
LENGTH:
1 m (max.)
STATUS:
Secure

Shovelnose rays are sometimes called "guitarfish" because their outline resembles that of a guitar. Like the closely related fiddler rays, the hind part of the body resembles a shark's (with a pair of high sail-like dorsal fins), but the front half is flattened and ray-like. Shovelnose rays have a long pointed snout that is used to dig prey from the sand bottom.

DESCRIPTION: Eastern Shovelnose Rays have a pale brown back, often with a pattern of darker brown blotches, and are white beneath. The snout is paler and may be translucent.

HABITAT: Eastern Shovelnose Rays are locally common in estuaries and off sandy beaches.

BEHAVIOUR: Shovelnose rays swim with side-to-side undulations of the tail, like a shark, and can give a flap of their pectoral fins to partly bury themselves in the sand and protect themselves from predators. Like most of the smaller rays, Eastern Shovelnose Rays are preyed upon by most large sharks.

FEEDING HABITS: This species is an active hunter. It feeds on crabs, molluscs and other sand-burrowing animals as well as small fish.

BREEDING: Male shovelnose rays have very long prominent claspers. After mating, the female produces egg cases containing 2–8 young that are retained internally until the small rays hatch. The young are then born alive, so this is a form of ovoviviparous development.

DANGER TO HUMANS: Shovelnose rays lack tail spines and are harmless to humans. This species is the target of a small commercial catch and is marketed as skate.

HABITAT & DISTRIBUTION:
Lives on sandy sea floors in water less than 50 m deep off NSW and southern Qld

SEXUAL MATURITY:
M & F approx. 65 cm

LENGTH:
1.2 m (max.)

STATUS:
Secure

This strange ray looks like a shark with a flattened head and large triangular pectoral fins. Shark Rays are very large and have high dorsal fins and a large tail fin that has a lower lobe almost the same size as the upper lobe. They have a broad, rounded snout that is distinctly separate from the pectoral fins and a number of spine-bearing ridges on the back and above the eyes.

DESCRIPTION: Shark Rays are blue-grey or brown-grey on the back with a mottled pattern of white spots. There is a crescent-shaped white-edged black blotch on the side of the head. The patterns become less distinct with age.

HABITAT: These unusual rays usually live on soft bottoms in shallow water but are also seen around reefs.

BEHAVIOUR: Although Shark Rays are often exhibited in large aquariums, little is known about this species' behaviour in the wild.

FEEDING HABITS: Shark Rays have flattened teeth grouped into crushing plates in both jaws — although teeth in the lower jaw are much larger than teeth in the upper jaw. Shark Rays feed primarily on crabs and shellfish that they dig from the bottom with their broad snout.

BREEDING: Very little is known about the breeding of Shark Rays but they probably give birth to live young that develop ovoviviparously.

DANGER TO HUMANS: This species has no tail spine. It is sometimes caught in prawn trawls, and a large individual can be difficult to remove.

HABITAT & DISTRIBUTION: Lives in shallow water on the coast and around reefs throughout the tropical Indo–West Pacific

SEXUAL MATURITY: Unknown
LENGTH: 2.7 m (max.)
WEIGHT: 130 kg (max.)
STATUS: Vulnerable (IUCN)

Whitespotted Guitarfish *Rhynchobatus australiae*

The Whitespotted Guitarfish is a large relative of the Shark Ray with a pointed, rather than rounded, snout. These two species are sometimes regarded, in various taxonomic circles, as sufficiently different from other guitarfish as to warrant their own order — Rhiniformes. This species has the same sail-like dorsal fins and crescent-shaped tail as the Shark Ray.

DESCRIPTION: These large guitarfish are grey or yellow-brown on the back with a pattern of white and black spots that may become indistinct in large adults. Behind the eye is a large breathing spiracle that has a distinctive double fold on the hind edge. There are lines of small blunt thorns down the middle of the back, on the shoulder and above the eye.

HABITAT: Whitespotted Guitarfish live around reefs or on sandy bottoms across northern Australia from Coffs Harbour to Fremantle.

BEHAVIOUR: These shark-like rays will often approach divers curiously and are quite active.

FEEDING HABITS: Whitespotted Guitarfish feed on a variety of bottom-living invertebrates and fish are caught using their plates of small scale-like teeth.

BREEDING: Little is known about the breeding habits of this species but it probably has ovoviviparous development like the other guitarfish.

DANGER TO HUMANS: Although they may weigh more than two men, these large guitarfish are considered harmless to humans.

HABITAT & DISTRIBUTION:
Lives over the continental shelf throughout northern Australia

SEXUAL MATURITY:
M & F 1.1 m

LENGTH: 3 m (max.)
WEIGHT: 220 kg (max.)
STATUS:
Vulnerable (IUCN)

Coffin Ray

The Coffin Ray is a small electric ray that packs a punch way out of proportion to its size. It has a powerful biological battery in each side of the body disc that can be switched on to deliver a strong electric shock to any animal nearby. These rays use electric shocks both to stun their prey and to frighten off potential predators.

DESCRIPTION: Coffin Rays have a rounded body disc and a short stumpy tail bearing two small dorsal fins. They have variable colour on the back, ranging from reddish-brown to chocolate brown, grey or pink with a few darker or paler spots and blotches. The belly is white.

HABITAT: Coffin Rays are usually found in shallow water on sand bottoms and around reefs. They are sometimes caught in trawl nets on the outer continental shelf.

BEHAVIOUR: Coffin Rays are slow-swimming and fearless, secure in their potent electrical defence!

FEEDING HABITS: These rays feed mainly at night using their small three-pronged teeth to eat crabs, worms and small fish that have been stunned into immobility.

BREEDING: Coffin Rays are viviparous and females give birth to 10 cm long live young.

DANGER TO HUMANS: Despite their chilling name, the electric shock produced by Coffin Rays is not fatal to humans. However, the shock is powerful enough to knock a person over and, once experienced, is not easily forgotten.

HABITAT & DISTRIBUTION: From close inshore to depths of over 200 m around south-eastern and western Australia

SEXUAL MATURITY: M & F 25 cm
LENGTH: 60 cm (max.)
STATUS: Secure

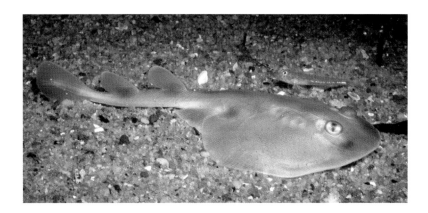

Numbfish belong to a group of electric rays that have a small, round body disc and relatively long tail. The electric shock from these rays is not as powerful as that of the Coffin Ray or the much larger Torpedo Electric Ray. At least five different species of numbfish live in Australian waters and all are endemic to our waters. Several of these species are still undescribed.

DESCRIPTION: The Tasmanian Numbfish is dark chocolate-brown on the back with paler fins and a white belly. These small rays have a paddle-shaped tail and a pair of equal-sized dorsal fins on the back of a long, shark-like tail.

HABITAT: These rays live on soft bottoms in shallow water around Tasmania but they are also found on the continental slope from 200–650 m deep in the warmer waters off northern New South Wales.

BEHAVIOUR: All Australian numbfish have small eyes and rely on senses other than vision for most of their activities. Some of their overseas relatives have non-functional eyes.

FEEDING HABITS: The Tasmanian Numbfish feeds mainly on crustaceans and other small invertebrates, as well as small fish — which it first stuns with electric shocks — whenever it can catch them.

BREEDING: Numbfish are ovoviviparous and have small litters of young that are less than 10 cm long when born.

DANGER TO HUMANS: Although numbfish can deliver an electric shock if they are handled, it is relatively weak compared with the shocks delivered by other electric rays.

HABITAT & DISTRIBUTION:
Lives on sand bottoms around south-eastern Australia

SEXUAL MATURITY:
M & F approx. 30 cm

LENGTH:
47 cm (max.)

STATUS:
Secure

Skates are rays with distinctive diamond-shaped bodies, usually with a pointed snout supported by a central nasal cartilage. Skates lack tail barbs but usually have many patches of sharp thorns on the back. The arrangement of these thorns is different for each of the 200 different skate species found worldwide. There are 38 skate species in Australia.

DESCRIPTION: Like all skates, this species has deeply notched pelvic fins, a pair of small dorsal fins near the tip of the tail and no tail fin. The Thornback Skate has a relatively thick, short tail and is brown on the back with darker blotches and mottling. It has a dark patch between the eyes and another on the underside of the snout tip.

HABITAT: Most skates live in deep water on the continental slope but the Thornback Skate lives in shallow water — preferring the muddy bottoms of bays and estuaries.

BEHAVIOUR: Like most rays, skates live on the seabed and often partially bury themselves beneath the sand to hide from predators.

FEEDING HABITS: These skates feed on small fish and crustaceans.

BREEDING: Male skates have a patch of retractable thorns on each wing that are probably used to grip the female during mating. All skates lay eggs that take several months to hatch. Thornback Skate young are born when they are about 15 cm long.

DANGER TO HUMANS: Skates are harmless, but their thorns can cause grazes and cuts if people handle these animals carelessly.

HABITAT & DISTRIBUTION:
On the shallow continental shelf around the south-eastern Australian coast

SEXUAL MATURITY:
M & F 40 cm
LENGTH:
52 cm (max.)
STATUS:
Secure

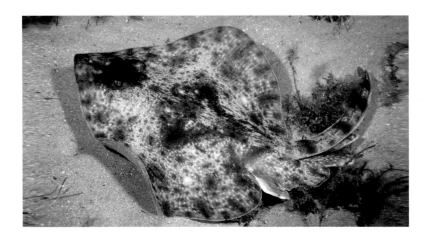

The Melbourne Skate is the largest of the Australian skates and grows to almost 2 m long. This species has a typical skate shape with a pointed snout and the normal two-lobed pelvic fins. The tail has three rows of long sharp thorns, one down the centre line and one on each side, and there are several thorns along the shoulders and back.

DESCRIPTION: Melbourne Skates are grey-brown on the back with a dense scattering of small white spots. Young individuals have large dark blotches on each side of the disc.

HABITAT: Melbourne Skates live on soft bottoms, usually in shallow water, but have been found as deep as 170 m.

BEHAVIOUR: Like most skates, little is known about their behaviour.

FEEDING HABITS: Melbourne Skates have many small teeth and feed on a variety of bottom-living animals including, shrimps, crabs, octopuses and small fish.

BREEDING: Males have very long claspers that are used to impregnate females when the skates gather together in large mating aggregations. All skates are oviparous, and females lay square egg cases that contain a single embryo. Egg cases have a horn on each corner that is attached to the bottom with sticky tendrils. Empty skate egg cases that are washed ashore have been given the name "mermaid's purses".

DANGER TO HUMANS: The thorny tail of these large skates can cause minor injuries when fishers attempt to remove them from nets or lines.

HABITAT & DISTRIBUTION:
On soft sea bottoms on the continental shelf across southern Australia

SEXUAL MATURITY:
M & F approx. 1 m
LENGTH: 1.7 m (max.)
WEIGHT: 50 kg
STATUS:
Secure

Whitespotted Eagle Rays are huge, almost rivalling Manta Rays in size, and have wide pointed "wings" like a Manta Ray. However, their strange pointed snout easily distinguishes them from their larger filter-feeding relatives. These rays have very long, thin tails that may be twice the body length (if they are undamaged), and one or two small spines on the upper tail-base like a stingray.

DESCRIPTION: Whitespotted Eagle Rays are graceful and beautiful when they are flying through the water. They have a green-grey back with a pattern of small white spots on the body and wings and a white belly.

HABITAT: These beautiful rays are often seen swimming around coral reefs in northern Australia.

BEHAVIOUR: Though most rays spend their lives lying on the sea floor, Whitespotted Eagle Rays spend most of their time swimming well above the bottom, often in large schools.

FEEDING HABITS: Whitespotted Eagle Rays have fused tooth plates in each jaw that are used to crush the shells of molluscs, such as clams and oysters, which these rays collect during their brief forays to the bottom.

BREEDING: During the mating season groups of males cooperate to hold onto a single female and take turns mating with her, belly to belly. Development of the young is ovoviviparous and pregnancy lasts twelve months. Litter size is 2–4 and the pups are 25 cm across when they are born.

DANGER TO HUMANS: These huge eagle rays are normally harmless but their spines may cause injuries if they are caught in a fishing net or line.

HABITAT & DISTRIBUTION:
Lives in shallow water around coral reefs to depths of 60 m in tropical and subtropical seas worldwide

SIZE:
3 m across; 9 m long (max.)
STATUS:
Near Threatened (IUCN)

Unlike their tropical cousins Southern Eagle Rays spend much of their lives on the bottom. Their huge pectoral fins are swept back and the body is wider than it is long. Like all eagle rays, they have a square snout that protrudes from the front of the body and easily distinguishes them from stingrays and stingarees. They have a relatively short stinging spine at the tail-base compared with stingrays.

DESCRIPTION: Southern Eagle Rays are olive-green to yellow-brown on the back, with a pattern of bluish spots and crescentic lines, and white on the belly.

HABITAT: Southern Eagle Rays are usually seen over open sand in shallow water but also hunt on rocky reefs.

BEHAVIOUR: Southern Eagle Rays look as though they are flying through the water as they flap their huge pectoral fins up and down like the wings of a bird. They appear to migrate further south in summer when the water is warmer.

FEEDING HABITS: These rays feed on molluscs and crabs that they crush with their tooth plates before swallowing. Shell fragments from their food are usually sorted from the meat and left in a neat pile on the bottom.

BREEDING: Southern Eagle Rays are ovoviviparous and give birth to young that are about 30 cm across.

DANGER TO HUMANS: These eagle rays have smaller spines than their stingray relatives, and are normally not aggressive, but should still be treated with caution. The Southern Eagle Ray is very similar to a species that is common around northern New Zealand, (*Myliobatis tenuicaudata*).

HABITAT & DISTRIBUTION:
Lives on sand and around rock reefs down to 85 m depth around southern Australia

SEXUAL MATURITY:
M & F approx. 80 cm

SIZE:
1.2 m across; 2 m long (max.)

STATUS:
Secure

Stingray Family

The typical stingray has a diamond-shaped body disc that incorporates the greatly enlarged and flattened pectoral fins and the smaller pelvic fins. They have a long whip-like tail with one or more large dagger-like spines on the upper surface near the tail-base. These spines have a needle-sharp tip and a serrated cutting edge with poison glands along each side.

DESCRIPTION: Many stingrays are large. The Smooth Stingray (*Dasyatis brevicaudata*) may have a body disc more than 2 m across, and weigh in excess of 350 kg. Stingrays have no dorsal, anal or tail fins but often have skin folds on the tail that look like fins.

HABITAT: Most stingrays live in sand or mud habitats and spend the majority of their lives resting on the bottom.

BEHAVIOUR: Stingrays swim by passing undulations down the sides of their body discs (with the wave on one side offset compared with that on the other). They often bury themselves in sediment, exposing only their eyes.

FEEDING HABITS: These rays expose their prey by blowing water through their mouth and gills or flapping their wings to move sand. They mainly feed on invertebrates such as molluscs, crustaceans, echinoderms and worms. Feeding activities leave characteristic pits in the sand, seen on sand flats at low tide or when snorkelling over sand.

BREEDING: Stingrays usually gather in groups to breed. Development of the young is viviparous and litter size is usually 2–6 young.

DANGER TO HUMANS: The protective stinging spine of large stingrays is like a stiletto blade, over 30 cm long, and makes a lethal weapon. It is wielded as a defence against large sharks but can cause fatal injuries to swimmers and divers if the stingray feels threatened.

Blotched Fantail Ray   *Taeniura meyeni*

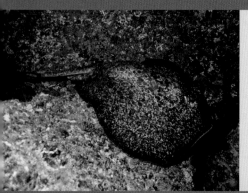

BIRTH SIZE: 35 cm across

SIZE: 1.8 m across; 3.3 m long (max.)

HABITAT & DISTRIBUTION: Lives in shallow water on sand and reefs throughout the tropical Indo–West Pacific

STATUS: Vulnerable (IUCN)

Bluespotted Maskray   *Dasyatis kuhlii*

SEXUAL MATURITY: 25 cm across

SIZE: 38 cm across; 67 cm long (max.)

HABITAT & DISTRIBUTION: Lives in inshore waters and on coral reefs throughout the tropical Indo–West Pacific

STATUS: Secure

Cowtail Stingray   *Pastinachus sephen*

BIRTH SIZE: 20 cm across

SIZE: 1.8 m across; 3 m long (max.)

HABITAT & DISTRIBUTION: Found in coastal waters and around reefs throughout the tropical Indo–West Pacific

STATUS: Secure

Black Stingray   *Dasyatis thetidis*

SIZE: 1.8 m across; 4 m long (max.)

WEIGHT: 210 kg (max.)

HABITAT & DISTRIBUTION: Lives on soft bottoms in temperate waters to 360 m depth around southern Australia, New Zealand and South Africa

STATUS: Secure

Stingaree Family

Stingarees are much smaller than the related stingrays and usually grow to 50–80 cm long, including the tail. The body disc of stingarees is often almost circular but some are more diamond-shaped. Their tails are shorter and fatter than the stingrays' and end in a true tail fin. They have a relatively long protective stinging spine about halfway down the tail, which has associated poison glands.

DESCRIPTION: There are about 22 different stingaree species found in Australian waters and about 40 species worldwide. Some stingaree species have a plain-coloured body disc but many of them have elaborate patterns of stripes, spots and blotches.

HABITAT: Stingarees are usually found in sand or mud habitats over the continental shelf but a few species may venture onto rocky reefs, while other species live in deeper water on the continental slope.

BEHAVIOUR: Most stingarees partially bury themselves in the sand to hide from predators when they are not actively hunting.

FEEDING HABITS: Bottom-living invertebrates such as molluscs, crustaceans, echinoderms and worms form the main food of stingarees.

BREEDING: The developing young are fed viviparously through yolk sac placentas in the female's uteruses. Litter size is only 2–4 and pregnancy lasts about three months.

DANGER TO HUMANS: Stingarees are usually small but have a large stinging spine for their size and can inflict painful wounds if they are touched or threatened.

Striped Stingaree *Trygonoptera ovalis*

SEXUAL MATURITY: M & F 35 cm

LENGTH: 60 cm (max.)

HABITAT & DISTRIBUTION: Soft bottoms down to 50 m around south-western Australia

STATUS: Secure

Yellowback Stingaree *Urolophus sufflavus*

SEXUAL MATURITY: M & F 23 cm

LENGTH: 42 cm (max.)

HABITAT & DISTRIBUTION: Lives on the outer continental shelf and upper slope in 50–300 m depth around temperate eastern Australia

STATUS: Vulnerable (IUCN)

Sparsely-spotted Stingaree
Urolophus paucimaculatus

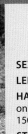

SEXUAL MATURITY: M & F 25 cm

LENGTH: 44 cm (max.)

HABITAT & DISTRIBUTION: Found on the continental shelf to depths of 150 m across southern Australia

STATUS: Secure

Banded Stingaree *Urolophus cruciatus*

SEXUAL MATURITY: M & F 25 cm

LENGTH: 50 cm (max.)

HABITAT & DISTRIBUTION: Lives in estuaries and shallow muddy bays to depths of 160 m around the coasts of southern Australia

STATUS: Secure

Manta Rays are all wings and mouth. The hugely expanded, swept-back pectoral fin "wings" dominate the body, with a thin tail trailing off the back, and a very wide mouth set on the front of the head. Long rounded flaps (known as cephalic lobes) protrude from the front of the head on each side of the mouth. These flaps help to funnel water into the wide-open mouth when these rays are feeding.

DESCRIPTION: Manta Rays are green-brown to dark grey on the back, and white with variable dark blotches on the belly. When not feeding, the huge mouth closes and the cephalic lobes are spirally folded, forming a straight horn to reduce drag.

HABITAT: Manta Rays are often seen on reef fronts or along current lines where plankton is concentrated.

BEHAVIOUR: Although Manta Rays are capable of crossing oceans, studies suggest that they rarely do. Many areas have small resident populations but in other locations Manta Rays make regular seasonal migrations between preferred feeding sites.

FEEDING HABITS: Manta Rays eat plankton filtered from the water that gushes through the open mouth and out the huge, distended gill slits. Stiff gill rakers in front of the gills trap plankton from the passing water. Large Mantas also eat small fish and have been known to join in shark feeding frenzies on bait fish.

BREEDING: Manta Rays usually give birth to a single young every two years. Manta Ray pups are about 1.3 m across at birth.

DANGER TO HUMANS: Although Manta Rays may weigh more than a tonne they are harmless to humans.

HABITAT & DISTRIBUTION:
Manta Rays are pelagic, usually living over the continental shelf in tropical seas worldwide

SIZE:
6.7 m across (max.)
WEIGHT:
1.5 t (max.)
STATUS:
Near Threatened (IUCN)

Above: A large Manta Ray feeds along a reef edge. Note the wide-open gill slits.

Chimaeras

These strange shark relatives are unusual in having a single pair of gill slits, like bony fish. They grub in soft bottom sediments for their food and have a dense network of sense organs on the nose and head that help them detect prey. All chimaeras are unusual among sharks in having a first dorsal fin that can be folded flat. A strong folding spine in front of this fin contains venom and is used for defence against predators. Chimaeras' pectoral fins are large and wing-like and are "flapped" to provide propulsion, with the tail being used for steering. Chimaeras have a small, rabbit-like mouth with beak-like cutting teeth, as well as crushing tooth plates. They feed on fish, squids and invertebrates. However, holding onto a female during mating is difficult with a small, rabbit-like mouth so male chimaeras have five claspers all equipped with spines, including a moveable, thumb-shaped clasper on top of the head, to help them to grip. After mating, female chimaeras move into shallow water and lay a pair of large, flanged eggs. Most chimaeras live on the continental slope in water ranging from 150-1400 m deep and are rarely seen by humans.

Top, left: Female Elephantfish carry a pair of large flanged egg cases around with them for a few days before depositing them on the bottom. **Below:** Strange longnose chimaeras in the family Rhinochimaeridae live in deep water on the continental slope.

Elephantfish *Callorhinchus milii*

Elephantfish are sometimes called Plough-nose Chimaeras. They are named for the plough-like extension on the tip of the nose that is used to dig in the bottom for food. This activity stirs up fine silt and reduces vision, so chimaeras rely on electroreception and an elaborate sensory system of pores and mucous canals on the head to detect food.

DESCRIPTION: The tail of Elephantfish is long and pointed and they have relatively high second dorsal and pelvic fins. They are silver-white in colour with dark blotches on the side.

HABITAT: Elephantfish are found on sand and mud bottoms around southern Australia but are most abundant in shallow Tasmanian waters.

BEHAVIOUR: These unusual fish often gather in loose schools and are usually shy when approached by divers.

FEEDING HABITS: Elephantfish have plate-like crushing teeth and a series of mouth papillae to help grip and sort the molluscs and invertebrates they feed on.

BREEDING: Females migrate into estuaries and inshore bays in spring to breed. They are oviparous and lay a pair of large golden eggs that are carried for a few days before being deposited on the bottom where they take 6–9 months to hatch. Elephantfish mature in 4–5 years and live for only 12–14 years.

DANGER TO HUMANS: The venomous fin-spine of these fish can inflict painful wounds if they are handled carelessly. Elephantfish are caught commercially around Tasmania and sold as "whitefish" fillets.

HABITAT & DISTRIBUTION:
Lives on the continental shelf to 200 m depth around temperate Australia and New Zealand

SEXUAL MATURITY:
M 65 cm; F 70 cm

LENGTH:
1.2 m (max.)

STATUS:
Secure

Glossary

AMPULLAE OF LORENZINI Receptors in the snouts of sharks, rays and chimaeras that permit detection of low-frequency electric stimuli to help them find food. These organs consist of a network of jelly-filled canals.

BARBELS Sensitive, whisker-like organs on the mouth, nostrils or chin of some fish, which aid in the search for food. Barbels hold very small taste buds and olfactory sensors.

BENTHIC (ZONE) Associated with, or living on, the bottom.

CEPHALIC LOBES Long head flaps on each side of a Manta Ray's mouth.

CLASPERS A tube-like part of the pelvic fin of male sharks and rays by which sperm are introduced to the female.

CONTINENTAL SHELF Part of the continent that lies under shallow seas.

COPEPOD Small crustaceans.

DERMAL DENTICLES Tooth-like scales of sharks and rays.

DORSAL (FINS) The fins on the backs of fish and sharks.

ELECTRORECEPTION The ability to receive and process electrical impulses from the surrounding environment.

ENDEMIC An animal or plant that can only be found in one particular location.

FLANGE A projecting rim, edge or flap.

HETEROCERCAL The most common tail shape among sharks: with two unequal sized lobes.

HOMOCERCAL A tail shape, in which both lobes are approximately equally sized.

IUCN International Union for the Conservation of Nature and Natural Resources.

NEUROMASTS Tiny hair cells inside a lateral line canal system, that help a shark "hear" vibrations in the water.

OVIPAROUS A method of reproduction in which eggs are laid by the female and develop outside her body. There is little or no embryonic development within the female.

OVOVIVIPAROUS A method of reproduction in which young develop in eggs that remain within the mother's body until hatching, and then are born as live offspring. From the Latin *ovum* (egg), *vivus* (alive) and *parere* (to produce). In many sharks the hatched embryos feed on a supply of unfertilised eggs produced continuously by the mother.

PECTORAL (FINS) The fins on the sides of fish and sharks.

PELAGIC Of the open ocean or animals living there.

PELVIC (FINS) The fins that are on the undersides of fish and sharks.

SHARK FINNING The practice of catching sharks just for their fins, which are prized as food in some countries. The mutilated body of the shark is often discarded.

SPIRACLE An opening in the heads of sharks and rays through which water is drawn and passed over the gills.

SQUALENE An oil that is found in sharks' livers.

UNDULATION A rippling motion.

VIVIPAROUS A method of reproduction where the developing embryos are fed through a placenta that is attached to the mother's uterine wall.

Index

Index continued

Links & Further Reading

Books

Aitken, K. *Green Guide: Sharks and Rays of Australia*, New Holland, Sydney, 1998

Allen, G. *Marine Fishes of Tropical Australia and South-East Asia*, Western Australian Museum, Perth, 1997

Hutchens, B. & Swainston, R. *Sea Fishes of Southern Australia*, Swainston Publishing, Perth, 1986

Kuiter, R. *Guide to Sea Fishes of Australia*, New Holland, Sydney, 1996

Kuiter, R. *Coastal Fishes of South-Eastern Australia*, University of Hawaii Press, Honolulu, 1993

Lieske, E. & Myers, R. *Coral Reef Fishes*, Princeton University Press, New Jersey, 2001

Randall, J., Allen, G. & Steene, R. *Fishes of the Great Barrier Reef and Coral Sea*, University of Hawaii Press, Honolulu, 1991

Stevens, J. & Last, P. *Sharks and Rays of Australia*, CSIRO Publishing, Canberra, 1991

Websites

Fish Base: A comprehensive worldwide database of shark, ray and fish taxonomy with distribution maps, descriptions and photos of 30,000 species. **www.fishbase.org**

Australian Museum Online: Ichthyology Section contains useful information on fish identification, biology and ecology. **www.austmus.gov.au/fishes/index.cfm**

United Nation FAQ Species Fact Sheets: Comprehensive illustrated data sheets for many fish and sharks. **www.fao.org/fi/website**

World Conservation Union Red List of Threatened Species. **www.iucnredlist.org/info/categories_criteria1994**

Biology of Sharks and Rays: A great website with lots of information on sharks and lots of illustrations. **www.elasmo-research.org**

International Shark Attack File: Statistics on worldwide shark attacks. **www.flmnh.ufl.edu/fish/Sharks/ISAF/ISAF.htm**

The lifestyle of fish. www.wetwebmedia.com/index.html

Australian Shark Attack File: Information on shark attacks in Australia. www.taronga.org.au/tcsa/conservation-programs/australian-shark-attack-file.aspx

Pictures and information on sharks and rays. **www.elasmodiver.com**

Wikipedia – the free encyclopedia: Has lots of information on sharks and rays but is occasionally unreliable. **www.en.wikipedia.org/wiki/Main_Page**

Great Barrier Reef Marine Park Authority: This website has a lot of useful information on the Great Barrier Reef and its ecosystems. **www.gbrmpa.gov.au**

Australian Museum Online: Ichthyology Section — useful information on fish identification, biology and ecology. **www.austmus.gov.au/fishes/index.cfm**

Australian Society for Fish Biology. **www.asfb.org.au**

Underwater Australasia: Lots of information on diving and fish. **www.underwater.com.au**

Opposite: Manta Ray (*Manta birostris*) feeding in current.

Published by Steve Parish Publishing Pty Ltd
PO Box 1058, Archerfield, Queensland 4108
Australia

www.steveparish.com.au

ISBN 978174193327 7

First published 2008

Photographer: Steve Parish

Additional photography: Kelvin Aitken/
Marine Themes: pp. 13 & 90 (bottom); Gary
Bell/Oceanwidelmages.com: pp. 5, 11 (top,
whale shark & human), 12, 33 (top), 45
(bottom), 55 (top), 57-8, 63, 82 & 87 (centre);
Bill Boyle/Oceanwidelmages.com:p.43 (top);
C & M FallowsOceanwidelmages. com:
pp. 33 (bottom), 35 & 64; Rudie Kuiter/
Oceanwidelmages.com: pp. 16, 19, 21, 38-9, 42
(bottom), 43 (centre & bottom), 45 (top), 68-9,
72, 79-81, 86 (top), 87 (top & bottom) & 90 (top);
Andy Murch/Oceanwidelmages.com:
pp. 23 (top), 34 (top), 36-7, 62, 71, 85 (centre) &
86 (bottom); Photolibrary: p. 60 (bottom); Ron
& Valerie Taylor: pp. 2 (bottom), 6 (top), 7-10, 15,
20, 22 (bottom), 23 (centre & bottom), 25 (top),
26, 27 (top), 28, 30-32, 44, 46-50, 51 (bottom), 53,
59, 60 (top), 61, 66, 70, 84 & 89

Illustrations: pp. 5 & 7,
Thomas Hamlyn-Harris, SPP

Front cover image: Grey Nurse Shark, Andy
Murch/Oceanwidelmages.com

Title page main image: Blacktip Reef Shark,
Gary Bell/Oceanwidelmages.com. Inset, top
to bottom: Southern Eagle Ray; White Shark's
teeth; Gary Bell/Oceanwidelmages.com.

Text: Dr Tony Ayling
Editorial: Ted Lewis; Sarah Lowe, Michele Perry,
& Helen Anderson, SPP
Design: Thomas Hamlyn-Harris,
Leanne Nobilio, SPP
Production: Tina Brewster, SPP

Prepress by Colour Chiefs Digital Imaging,
Brisbane, Australia
Printed in Singapore by Imago

**Produced in Australia at the Steve Parish
Publishing Studios**